Bolton's Best

Venison Sausage Seasoning

Venison Jerky Marinade

Specially formulated and blended to bring out the best in venison jerky and sausage. Prepared and packaged under the most stringest quality standards

Perfectly seasons 25 pounds of venison

Send the order blank below to Seacoast Seasonings, P.O. Box 26492, Birmingham, Alabama 35226. Your spices will be immediately shipped to you. Please enclose your check with your order. Sorry, no CODs.

Please send me
____ package of Venison Sausage seasoning at $2.50 per package
____ packages of Venison Jerky Marinade at $2.50 per package. Price includes all shipping and handling.
Please send them to:
Name:_____
Street:_____
City, State, Zip:_____
Telephone: (___)_____

Preparing and Cooking

Alabama's Wild Game

By Mike Bolton
Outdoors Editor
The Birmingham News

Alabama's Wild Game _____

Other books by Mike Bolton
The Complete Alabama Fisherman
Mike Bolton's Favorite Alabama Jokes
Mike Bolton's Favorite Auburn Jokes

Published by
Seacoast Publishing, Inc.
P.O. Box 26492
Birmingham, Alabama 35226

Copyright 1992 by Mike Bolton

All rights reserved. No part of this book may be reproduced in any form by any means without the prior written permission of the publisher, except brief quotes used in reviews or articles written for magazines, newsletters or newspapers.

Printed in the United States of America

ISBN 1-878561-07-3

 Alabama's Wild Game

To my hunting buddies Rocco Lorino, David Ballard and Carl Mancha. They never met a meal they didn't like.

Alabama's Wild Game

Index

Introduction/7
Armadillo Recipes/13
Dressing Armadillos/17
Beaver Recipes/19
Dressing Beaver/24
Dove Recipes/27
Dressing Dove/36
Duck Recipes/39
Dressing Duck/42
Frog Leg Recipes/45
Dressing Frogs/48
Goose Recipes/51
Dressing Geese/54
Muskrat Recipes/57
Dressing Muskrat/60
Possum Recipes/63
Dressing Possum/66
Quail Recipes/69
Dressing Quail/76
Rabbit Recipes/79
Dressing Rabbit/84
Raccoon Recipes/87
Dressing Raccoon/92
Rattlesnake Recipes/87
Dressing Rattlesnake/100

Squirrel Recipes/103
Dressing Squirrel/106
Wild Turkey Recipes/109
Dressing Wild Turkey/112
Turtle Recipes/115
Dressing Turtle/117
Venison Recipes/119
Field Dressing Deer/133
Aging Venison/134
Skinning A Deer/134
Butchering A Deer/135
Deboning Venison/136
Venison On The Hoof/137
Venison Cuts/138
Venison Jerky Recipes/140
Making Venison Sausage/142
Woodchuck Recipes/147
Dressing Woodchuck/150

Alabama's Wild Game

Author Mike Bolton, left, and Buckmasters founder Jackie Bushman pose with deer that Bolton took to win 1992 Buckmasters Classic

Introduction

One of the truly enjoyable rewards of my life in Alabama's great outdoors has been sharing that experience with family and friends by feeding them from the bounty I have harvested.

One of my greatest joys is to watch an apprehensive face tasting wild game for the first time suddenly burst into a smile, followed by comments like "I never dreamed ..."

Alabama provides a wide array of delicacies guaranteed to please even the most discerning palate. Whether it be an elegant recipe like champagne quail, or just plain baked venison, the potential is there for the best meal you ever eat to come from Alabama's wild.

The importance of proper care

Chances are that your great-grandfather and great-great-grandfather were proficient at putting wild game on the dinner table. Chances are they were also proficient at putting domesticated meats such as beef and pork on the table, too.

They were likely experts on all aspects of the experience including killing, dressing, cutting up, curing, wrapping and storing the meat. They understood the importance of properly caring for the potential meal all the way from the gunshot to the dinner table.

Alabama's Wild Game

I mention that because times have changed. Most Alabamians now eat only domesticated meats that are bought at the local grocery store. These animals - mostly cattle, swine, chicken and turkey - are killed, butchered, wrapped, cooled and frozen under strict USDA control. It's a safe bet that the meat you purchase from your local grocer is as fresh as it can be when you take it from the store.

Today, less than 10 percent of Alabamians have hunting licenses. You don't have to be much of a mathematician to see only a small percentage of state residents ever eat game.

Unfortunately, too few of those who hold hunting licenses are experts on the proper care of the meat from the shot to the table. I'm often appalled at the number of excellent hunters I see who are uneducated to the point of being dangerous in their handling and serving of wild game.

I've eaten my share of foul-tasting wild game and met many people who have eaten wild game who now gag at the thought of eating more. Most complain about wild game's "bloody" or "gamey" taste. These unfortunate souls have no doubt been done a terrible injustice from an outdoorsman who didn't properly care for, or prepare, his game or catch. These poor souls probably were served spoiled meat.

Suppose you were to shoot a cow, drag the whole cow through the woods unbutchered, throw up in the back of a truck and drive it around town showing it to your friends for a few hours before butchering it. If you were then to serve it to someone who has never eaten beef before, you would then be told beef has a "gamey" taste.

I always cringe at the statement that a certain wild game is "good if it's cooked right." That's usually a tip-off someone is getting meat that wasn't properly cared for. Wild game and fish have a unique flavor, but it isn't a bad flavor that needs to be disguised by overcooking and heavy seasoning. Why bother hide the flavor of the meat? If you want something that doesn't taste like wild game, go the grocery store and buy a Hostess Twinkie.

A few rules

I dwell on the importance of the proper care of wild game for two reasons. First, failing to do so can be dangerous. Food poisoning and internal parasites are results of improper care. Two, first impressions are lasting and it usually takes only one bad-tasting meal for a would-be game eater to never attempt it again. If it's your family refuses to eat game, you may be forced to give away literally thousands of dollars of "free" (I use that term loosely) meat that your family could have enjoyed.

Proper preparation starts the minute you pull the trigger. With wild game, the best way to avoid spoilage is to cool the meat as soon as possible; keep it clean and away from insects. Internal organs should be removed as soon as possible.

If the game is venison, and you're more than 30 minutes from camp, field dress the animal immediately. If possible, drag the deer to the shade, preferably on a hillside (more of this in the section on venison) and remove the internal organs. Prop open the body cavity to enhance air circulation. Then get the animal to the dressing shed.

Never go into the woods without a ride out. Hunters who are dropped out before daylight and won't be picked up until 10:30 or 11 a.m., aren't hunters. They're sleepers. If the weather is warm, and it usually is much of the Alabama deer season, a deer shot at 6 a.m. and not dressed to noon is a disaster.

If the game is birds, squirrels or rabbits, don't throw them in the back of a hunting vest for long periods of time. Plan ahead. Have a cooler with ice somewhere nearby. If you're going to be in the field for long periods, take periodic breaks to take a trip to the cooler. Remove the animals' organs and put the birds or animals on ice.

Have the right equipment

Too many hunters and fishermen spend thousands of dollars on equipment and spend hundreds of hours on preparations and then walk into the woods without a clue on what to do with their bounty if they are successful. Make part of your hunting equipment the right equipment for field dressing.

If you spend $800 for a good rifle and scope, $3,000 for a 4-wheeler and $500 annually for a membership into a hunting club, why skimp on a good skinning knife and cooler?

My best purchase ever was a 200 quart Gott cooler several years ago. This insulated cooler has brought home its share of cut-up deer, dove, quail, rabbit and squirrel and deposited them

Alabama's Wild Game

at my doorstep in excellent condition.

I keep it in the back of my truck full of wrapping paper, wrapping tape, felt-tipped markers (for marking different cuts of kinds of meat) and knives, sharpeners and meat saws whenever I'm hunting.

The best trick I've learned is to use the big cooler for my dove stool. Much of Alabama's dove hunting season, and especially that in September, is hot. I put in my customary five bags of ice, plus two gallon milk jugs full of water, a box of sandwich bags, a pair of scissors, lunch, and soft drinks.

Whenever I shoot a dove, instead of throwing it on the ground or putting it in the back of my shooting vest, I pull the breast loose with my index finger, then clip the wing bones loose with the scissors. I wash the breast in a little water, then place it in a sandwich bag and immediately put it on ice.

Never doubt dove spoil easily in September, and even in October and November. My method keeps them fresh.

Here's some more equipment you will need:

Knives - Knives come in many shapes, sizes and prices. There is no universal knife, so don't let anyone tell you there is.

For hunters, an expensive, folding knife with a lockable blade is best. Avoid the Bowie-type knives that may look cool when they are strapped to your leg. All that does is tip off fellow hunters that you are either a moron or from north of the Mason-Dixon line.

Keep in mind the knife will often be working in close quarters, it needs to cut with the precision of a surgical instrument; it often will be misused as a bone saw. The knife will have to be resharpened often and it will need to be washed under running water regularly.

That's quite a demand, and not one that is going to be met by a $10 pocket knife or a knife purchased from a late-night TV ad. Check with someone who butchers deer regularly and see what they use, then buy from a reputable sporting goods store.

I also keep a filet knife on hand. It comes in handy not only for fish, but also for many delicate cuts, such a removing dove breast meat from the bone and cutting out venison backstraps and tenderloins.

Knife sharpener - Keeping a knife sharp is of utmost importance and for more reasons than the obvious one of making work easier. Almost every accident I've seen when someone cut themselves dressing game animals has had two common denominators: (1) the person who was injured was tired after a long day of hunting, and (2) he was forcing cuts with a dull knife.

It's an old cliche that dull knives cut more people than sharp knives, but it's a fact. A sharp knife glides through cuts with ease and results in much less wasted meat. Don't skimp on a knife sharpener.

A stone is the tried and true method of sharpening a knife, and is an excellent way of keeping the blade sharp. Purchase a good stone and follow the directions that came with the knife on how to keep it sharp.

There are several other types of good knife sharpeners on the market. Inquire at your local sportings goods store.

Saws - If you dress venison, you'll need a saw of some sort to cut through bone. A professional bone saw like butchers use is nice, but expensive. So are replacement blades. Such saws usually sell for $50 or more with blades costing $15 or more. A bone saw is a good investment for a hunting club which will dress many deer through the years, however.

A hack saw will suffice. Keep plenty of extra blades on hand because you'll break a few. Fine-toothed blades like that used to cut aluminum are perfect.

Pliers - It's always good to have a pair of pliers around. Put a pair of slip-joint pliers and needle-nose pliers in your dressing kit. You'll need both more than you think.

Old scissors - I keep a pair of old scissors in my cooler and, like pliers, you will always need them for something. They are excellent for cutting wing bones of dove, quail and ducks, not to mention freezer paper and freezer tape.

Hatchet - You'll use a hatchet for a variety of dressing chores.

Wrapping supplies - Freezer paper is a must if you're a deer hunter. Too many hunters take great pains in dressing their deer, only to throw it in a cooler full of bloody ice water for the ride home. You would have a heart attack if the meat manager at your local grocer cut you some nice steaks and packed them in ice water. Why is venison different? Double wrap your venison cuts with freezer paper, secure with freezer tape and label the cuts with a felt tip marker. Do the same with all game you plan to leave in the freezer for more than two weeks.

Smaller game that you plan to eat within two weeks can be

Alabama's Wild Game

placed in resealable bags. Don't pack in ice water, however.

Gimbrel - A gimbrel is a metal device that slides through the split tendons in a deer's rear legs and is used to hoist a deer off the ground. A gimbrel in invaluable. If you have access to a welder you can build your own, or you may purchase one for $20 or less at a sporting goods or hardware store.

Meat hammer - If you dress deer, purchase a meat hammer at your local grocery store. The cost is less than $5 and it's worth the price for tenderizing meat.

Sausage grinder - If you're a deer hunter who eats venison, put a sausage grinder on your list of musts. You can use it for both sausage and ground venison. A hand-cranked sausage grinder usually costs less than $30.

Armadillo

After spending 100 years working its way from Mexico and south Texas, the nine-banded armadillo finally reached extreme south Alabama in the 1940's. Along the way, the armadillo learned not only would Louisiana Cajuns turn them into turnpike pizza with the family automobile, they would also throw them into a boiling pot.

The armadillo has spent the past 50 years moving northward in Alabama and by 1992 reached as far northwest as Jasper and as far northeast as Heflin. He is most common in the blackbelt where he often drives hunters crazy with his noisy walk through the woods.

The armadillo is often called "'possum on the half-shell" by some Alabamians, but the nasty-looking animal makes a raw oyster look like Miss Alabama.

Although the armadillo has firmly established itself in Alabama's road kill hall-of-fame, it has by no means become common tablefare. Don't let anyone tell you that if fixed right, armadillos are a delicacy. They ain't. But they are edible and saying that you have eaten an armadillo brings a respect akin to saying you have jumped out of an airplane.

Alabama's Wild Game

Armadillo recipes

Barbecued Armadillo

1 teaspoon crab boil
1 stick of butter
1 cup barbecue sauce
1 tablespoon Liquid Smoke
2 tablespoons Dale's Steak Seasoning

Remove the shell and skin and wash thoroughly. Soak the armadillo in salty water overnight in the refrigerator. Cut the armadillo into pieces like chicken. Place in covered pot and cover with water and add crab boil. Boil for 30 minutes or until tender. Remove and brown in butter, then place in a shallow baking dish and brush on mixture of melted butter, Dale's Steak Seasoning, Liquid Smoke and barbecue sauce. Bake at 300° for one hour. Baste every 20 minutes. Serves 2.
Judge George Warner, Meridian, Miss.

Grey Poupon Armadillo

1 armadillo, cut up
1 large onion, diced
1 cup cheap white wine
1 tablespoon Argo cornstarch
1 stick of butter
Garlic salt, to taste
Salt and pepper, to taste
1/2 cup Grey Poupon mustard
1/2 cup peanut oil
2 cups cream
2 tablespoons Dale's Steak Seasoning

Combine oil, cheap wine, salt and pepper, garlic salt, onion and Dale's Steak Seasoning to make marinade. Add cutup pieces of armadillo to marinade and place in refrigerator overnight. Turn meat over in marinade before breakfast. Remove armadillo and set marinade aside. Melt butter in deep iron skillet and brown pieces. Pour marinade over brown pieces, cover, and simmer until tender. Remove pieces and set marinade aside. Place

Alabama's Wild Game

armadillo pieces on platter in warm oven. Mix Grey Poupon and cornstarch, then mix in cream. Return skillet and marinade mixture to low heat and add mustard mixture a little at a time. Stir sauce, without boiling, until it thickens. Pour sauce over armadillo pieces and serve on wild rice. Serves 2.

Armadillo in Tomato Gravy

2 armadillos, cut up
2 cans whole tomatos, mashed
2 sticks celery, chopped
2 medium onions, diced
1 banana pepper, chopped
1 stick margarine
1 tablespoon cornstarch
1 tablespoon Dale's Steak Seasoning
1 small can button mushrooms
1/2 cup red wine
Salt and pepper to taste

Melt margarine in Dutch oven and add vegetables. Set juice from tomatos and mushrooms aside. Saute approximately 4 minutes over medium heat. Add wine and juice from mushrooms and tomatos. Add armadillo pieces to Dutch oven and cover. Simmer for approximately 30 minutes, adding water when necessary. Remove armadillo pieces and add flour and Dale's Steak Seasoning to make gravy. Add mushrooms. Cook gravy until thick and pour over armadillo. Serves 4.

Alabama's Wild Game

Oriental Armadillo

1 armadillo, deboned and cubed
1 can water chestnuts
4 large onions, chopped
1 stalk celery, chopped
1/2 pound fresh mushrooms, sliced
1/4 cup Dale's Steak Seasoning
2 cups rice, uncooked
salt and pepper to taste
2 quarts water

Boil armadillo cubes in salted water until tender. Remove armadillo meat and set broth aside. In dutch oven, cook onions and celery in hot oil until tender. Add mushrooms, water chestnuts and meat and saute 5 minutes. Add 6 cups of hot broth, rice, salt and pepper and Dale's Steak Seasoning, stir. Simmer until rice is done. Serves 8.

Baked Armadillo

1 armadillo, cut up
1 stick margarine
1/4 cup Dale's Steak Seasoning
1 cup Zesty Italian salad dressing
1/2 cup white vinegar
1/4 cup lemon juice
1 teaspoon onion salt
1/2 teaspoon garlic salt
1/2 teaspoon lemon pepper

Melt margarine in saucepan and add all ingredients, stirring well. Remove armadillo pieces to foil-lined baking pan. Pour sauce over meat. Flip meat over several times to make sure it is well coated. Cover with foil. Bake at 325° for 45 minutes.

Dressing armadillo

Get the armadillo ready for the dinner table by first shooting his ugly head off. Don't shoot the body, because this will drive pieces of the hard shell deep into the meat and you won't find them until a filling falls out. Use a skinning knife (diagram 1) to cut off the the head, the tail and feet. Flip the armadillo over on its back (diagram 2) and run the knife under the shell and remove it. You'll then have something like a baby pig with a few hairs around each leg. Slit the belly from the neck to the anus (diagram 3) and remove insides. Scald the meat in boiling water. Remove any fat. Cut into pieces.

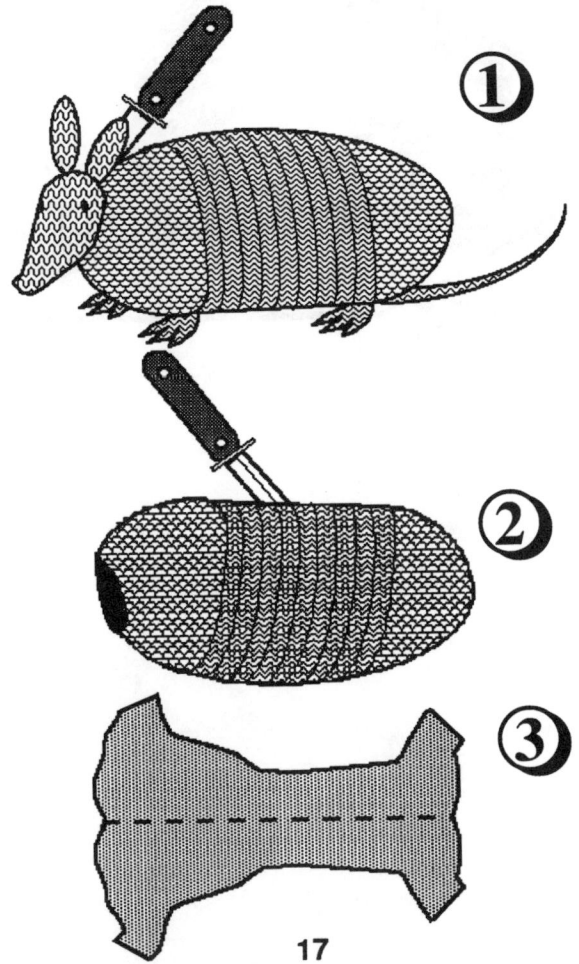

Alabama's Wild Game _____

Beaver

Beavers are abundant in Alabama. So abundant, in fact, several Alabama counties place a bounty on their heads.

Because of crude firearms that made the shooting of deer and turkey a difficult chore, the beaver, which was trapped, was a staple meet of Colonists as they left the Eastern Seaboard and began branching out westward.

Beaver are easy to obtain in Alabama. Most pond and lake owners who have them on their property are usually more than willing to allow a hunter to sit and wait on them as they appear on the pond or lake at daybreak and again just before sunset. A .22-caliber rifle is an excellent weapon choice.

Trapping also is an excellent way to acquire beaver. Trappers trap them for their hides and usually dispose of the remainder of the animal. A call to a local conservation officer, or county agent, can usually result in a phone number of a local trapper.

Beaver is rich, dark and has the same texture of beef. It makes excellent shish kabobs, stew meat and barbecue. Of all of the truly unusual wild game that swims in Alabama, many believe beaver is the best.

The bad news is that beaver fat is overpowering in odor and taste, and if you get it on your hands, it will stay there for a few days. Once skinned, a beaver smells like a bathroom on a shrimp boat, so dress him outside and away from the house.

Alabama's Wild Game

Recipes

Basic Beaver

1 young beaver (no gray hair) cut into pieces
2 tablespoons Dale's Steak Seasoning
2 tablespoons Liquid Smoke
Lowery's Seasoned Salt
1/4 cup bacon drippings
1 cup of water
Flour

Sprinkle serving-size pieces of beaver with seasoned salt. Mix Dale's, Liquid Smoke and water in large cast iron skillet and bring to simmer. Add beaver pieces to skillet and cook until tender. Remove. Clean skillet, add bacon drippings and re-heat. Batter cooked pieces of beaver in flour and return to skillet. Fry to a golden brown.

Barbecued Beaver

1 young beaver, deboned and cubed
1/2 gallon apple juice
seasoning salt
favorite barbecue sauce

Marinate 1-inch cubes of beaver in apple juice overnight. Remove cubes and set apple juice aside. Place cubes on skewer and cook on grill until well done, basting often with apple juice. Brush on barbecue sauce for the final 5 minutes of cooking time.

Fried Beaver Tail No. 1

1 beaver tail, skinned
2 cups of water
1 cup of vinegar
1 egg, beaten
Flour
Vegetable oil

Alabama's Wild Game

Simmer tail in water and vinegar for 1 1/2 hours. Drain and cut meat into strips. Dip meat into beaten egg, then flour, fry in a hot skillet until golden brown.

Fried Beaver Tail No. 2

2 beaver tails
1/2 cup white vinegar
1 tablespoon salt
2 tablespoons baking soda
1/2 teaspoon salt
1/4 teaspoon pepper
1/4 cup flour
1 stick margarine
1/2 cup dry sherry
1 teaspoon dry mustard
1 teaspoon sugar
1/4 teaspoon garlic powder
1 tablespoon Dale's Steak Seasoning

Skin beaver tails and cut up into serving-sized pieces. Soak beaver tail meat overnight in cold water, adding vinegar and 1 tablespoon of salt to water. Remove tails and rinse. Add baking soda to water to 2 quarts of water. Put the beaver tails in water and bring to a boil. Reduce heat and simmer 10 minutes. Season with salt and pepper and batter in flour before sauteing in pan of melted butter. Cook over medium heat until tender. Make sauce from sherry, mustard, garlic, sugar and Dale's. Add slowly to beaver tails and simmer 10 more minutes, basting often.

Alabama's Wild Game

Grilled Beaver Tail

1 beaver tail.
1 stick margarine
1/4 teaspoon garlic salt
Salt and pepper to taste

Wash beaver tail, but do not skin. Cut tail in half. Make sauce by melting margarine in saucepan and adding ingredients. Place beaver tail on grill, cover with foil and cook until tail splits open. Pull back skin and brush on sauce. Eat with a fork. One beaver tail feeds two people.

Baked Beaver

2 beaver loins
1 large can V8 vegetable juice
2 medium onions, chopped
2 tablespoons Dale's Steak Seasoning
Garlic salt, to taste
Seasoning salt, to taste
Black pepper, to taste
Vegetable oil

Sprinkle loins with garlic salt, seasoning salt and black pepper. Brown in hot oil, adding onions at the end. Add V8 juice and Dale's. Cover and bake at 350° for 1 1/2 hours.

Roast Beaver

1 medium-size beaver, skinned
2 onions, sliced
4 large potatoes, quartered
Flour
Corn starch
Garlic salt, to taste
Paprika, to taste
Seasoning salt, to taste
2 tablespoons Liquid Smoke
1 cup Dale's Steak Seasoning

Alabama's Wild Game

Remove all fat from animal. Cut meat into serving-size pieces. Sprinkle pieces with garlic salt and paprika. Coat pieces in flour and corn starch. Fry until golden brown. Place in roaster. Add remaining ingredients to roaster and place 1 inch of water in roaster. Roast for 2 hours at 375°.

Mike Bolton

Beaver Goulash

10 lbs. beaver meat, cubed
2 lbs. lean ground chuck
1 lb. bacon
2 lb. okra, sliced
2 lb. Lima beans
3 large onions, chopped
10 medium tomatos, peeled and crushed
Salt and pepper
1 cup of Dale's Steak Seasoning
Flour

Cook beaver meat in pressure cooker until tender. Brown ground chuck in skillet and pour off grease. Slice bacon in 1-inch pieces and fry in same skillet. Save bacon grease. Combine beaver, ground chuck and bacon in a large pot and add onions, okra, Lima beans, tomatos and Dale's. Season with with salt and pepper. Simmer for 2 hours, adding thickening paste made from flour mixed with bacon grease the final 30 minutes.

Alabama's Wild Game _____

Dressing beaver

Start by removing the beaver's tail (diagram 1, cut No. 1). This can be done with a knife and bone saw, but a hatchet will speed up the work. Flip the beaver over and cut off the feet (cuts No. 2 & 3). Split the pelt (cut No. 4) from the neck to the tail, being careful to keep the knife under the skin without puncturing the stomach. Use pliers to pull the skin away from the stomach and breast (diagram No. 2). Carefully split the skin and allow the insides to fall out. Cut all the insides away. Flip the beaver back over on its stomach (diagram No. 3) and carefully remove the remainder of the pelt by holding the pelt away from the body and cutting between the pelt and skin with short strokes. You will set that the rancid fat is everywhere. This is the fat that protects the beaver from the icy cold water. Rinse the beaver thoroughly with a water hose, being careful not to touch the fat.

Fill a 48-quart ice chest with water and add 1 box of baking soda, 1 cup of salt and 1 cup of vinegar. Place the beaver in the cooler and soak it overnight. The beaver will emerge in the morning smelling fresh. Scrape and cut all the white fat off the red meat and cut the beaver into cooking-size pieces and he's ready to cook.

Alabama's Wild Game

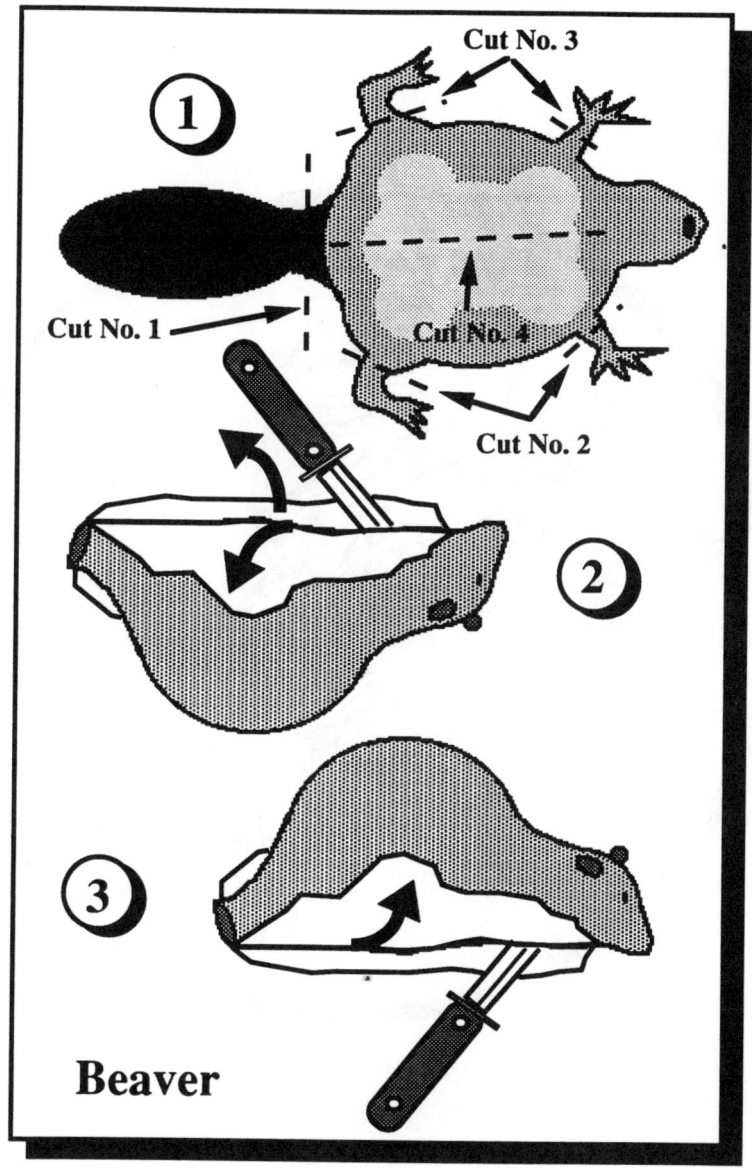

Beaver

Alabama's Wild Game _____

Dove

For many Alabama hunters, the most exciting time of the year is the opening of dove season. It not only comes at the end of a long, hot summer and signals that cooler weather is just around the corner, it also offers the first chance to go hunting in the new season. There's just something special about cleaning the old shotgun again, digging out the camouflage and knowing wild game will be on the table again soon.

The mourning dove, so named because of its sad and unmistakable, *coo, coo* call, can make two claims: It's the most-often "shot and missed" game in Alabama and it's the most ill-handled on the way to the dinner table.

Both of those problems are correctable.

Most of Alabama's better dove hunters take to the skeet fields at least a few weeks before heading to the dove field on opening day. This helps bring back the "touch" of the unnatural act of placing a shotgun to your shoulder and making it shoot where it should, specifically, at a darting, fast-flying bird approximately the size of a 16-ounce soft drink bottle.

This bit of practice goes a long way in not only saving expensive shotgun shells, it tends to help save a bit of face, too.

The Alabama dove season opens in September and it's always hot, which places a major emphasis on proper handling techniques for the birds once they are down. All too many hunters toss the birds in a pile until the days end, which not only

Alabama's Wild Game

encourages spoilage, it also invites ants and other insects.

I solved that problem a long time ago by learning that my Gott 200-quart cooler is both an excellent place to keep my birds cool and a great seat. I fill my cooler with five bags of ice, two 1-gallon milk jugs of water, a box of sandwich bags, a pair of scissors, lunch and soft drinks, a piece of camouflage cloth, a hand towel and my shells.

I take my cooler to the field on the back of a truck, and once there, I place it at a pre-scouted location, usually under a good shade tree. I then place the camouflage cloth on top of the cooler and take a seat.

Whenever I shoot a dove, instead of throwing them on the ground or putting them in the back of my shooting vest, I toss them into the cooler. Every so often, I take a break and pull the dove breasts loose with my index finger, then clip the wing bones with the scissors. I wash the breasts in a little water, then place them in sandwich bags and immediately put them on ice.

Not everyone wants to carry around a 200-quart cooler, so you may consider a 48-quart cooler. It will work, also.

Doves spoil easily not only in September, but October and November, too. Handle them with the care you would show any piece of meat you would put on your table.

Dove recipes

Mike Bolton's Dove Shish Kebobs

This a recipe we picked up in Station de Santa Engracia, a small Mexican town in the State of Tamulipas, while whitewing dove hunting several years ago. It was intended for whitewing dove - Paloma ala blanca, as the natives call it - but it works just as well for mourning dove. We substituted Dale's Seasoning Sauce for worcestershire sauce.

15 doves breasts, filleted
8 slices of bacon
5 medium onions, quartered
1 pound fresh mushrooms
3 bell peppers
1 pound cherry tomatos
1/4 cup cooking sherry
2 tablespoons Dale's Steak Sauce
1/4 cup white vinegar
1/4 ceaspoon garlic salt.

Marinate dove breast halves in cooking sherry, Dale's, vinegar and garlic salt overnight. Save mixture. Wrap each dove half in 1/4 slice of bacon. Place dove, onion, dove, bell pepper, tomato, dove, mushroom, dove - in that order - on skewers and place on grill. Sprinkle with seasoning salt. Brush often with remaining marinade.

Mike and Beth Bolton

Alabama's Wild Game

Basic Fried Dove

15 dove breasts
2 eggs, beaten
1/2 cup milk
2 1/2 cups pancake mix
Salt and pepper to taste
Vegetable oil

Season dove breasts with salt and pepper. Dip breasts in mixture of egg and milk. Batter in pancake mix and deep fry in vegetable oil. Doves are ready when they float to top. Don't overcook.

Gravy Doves

15 dove breasts
1/2 cup water
1 package chicken gravy mix
Salt and pepper to taste
2 tablespoons margarine

Place dove breasts in foil-lined 8-inch square pan. Sprinkle water over breasts. Sprinkle with gravy mix and salt and pepper. Dot with margarine. Seal foil tightly and bake at 350° for one hour.

Creamed Dove Breasts

15 dove breasts
1/2 cup flour
2 chicken bouillon cubes
1 medium onion, sliced
Salt and pepper to taste
1/4 cup whole milk

Salt and pepper dove breasts. Flour and brown in oil in skillet. Remove dove and drain on paper towel. Pour excess oil from skillet. Add flour to remaining skillet drippings to make gravy. After paste begins to brown, add water to desired thickness. Add crushed chicken bouillon to gravy. Put doves back in pan with gravy and top with onion. Add milk and stir. Cover and cook over low heat for 1 hour.

Alabama's Wild Game

Smothered Dove Breasts

15 dove breasts, filleted
2 large onions, chopped
6 slices bacon, fried and crumbled
1 1/2 sticks margarine
1 bell pepper, chopped
1/2 cup chopped mushrooms
4 stalks celery, chopped
Garlic salt, to taste
Salt and pepper to taste
Flour
Oregano, to taste
Sage, to taste
Thyme, to taste

Batter breast halves in flour. Sprinkle with sage. Melt 1 stick margarine in skillet and brown battered halves on both sides. Remove dove meat and drain on paper towels. Add onions, celery, mushrooms and bell pepper and cook on low heat until onions become opaque. Return meat to skillet and add 1/2 stick of margarine, bacon, garlic salt, thyme, oregano and sage. Simmer for 10 minutes. Serve over wild rice.

Baked Dove Hawaiian

15 dove breasts
15 bacon strips
1 16-ounce can crushed pineapple
1 medium green pepper, chopped
1 small onion, chopped
salt and pepper, to taste
3 tablespoons melted butter

Combine pineapple, green pepper and onion. Salt and pepper the dove breasts. Wrap each breast in a strip of bacon and secure with toothpicks. Place doves in 9x13 baking dish. Pour pineapple mixture over doves and bake at 325 degrees for 45 minutes.
Alabama Cooperative Extension Service, Auburn University

Southern Roasted Dove Breasts

12 dove breasts
Juice of 2 lemons
Salt and pepper, to taste
3/4 cup worcestershire sauce
12 bacon slices
1 12-ounce can frozen orange juice

Place dove breasts in a large bowl. Make a marinade of lemon juice, salt, pepper and worcestershire sauce and pour over doves. Cover and let marinate in the refrigerator overnight. Remove from marinade, wrap each breast with toothpick. Place in a roasting pan and pour orange juice over doves. Bake at 350 degrees 30 to 45 minutes or until tender.
Alabama Cooperative Extension Service, Auburn University

Braised Doves

8 dove breasts
Flour
Cornmeal
Vegetable oil
Water
Salt and pepper, to taste

Salt and pepper dove breasts and powder with flour and cornmeal. Brown breasts in oil. Remove breasts and drain on paper towel. Pour oil out of skillet. Add 1/4 inch of water to skillet; cover and simmer for 45 minutes over low heat.

Dove Pie

6 doves, cleaned and split
32 ounces of water
1 onion, chopped
1 small bunch parsley, chopped
3 whole cloves
2 tablespoons flour
2 tablespoons margarine
Salt and pepper, to taste

Pie pastry

Cover doves with water; add onion, parsley and cloves. Cook until tender, about 15 minutes. Removes doves and skim liquid. Thicken liquid with paste made of flour and margarine. Season with salt and pepper. Remove from heat. Line a baking dish with pastry. Place cooked birds in dish. Cover with gravy. Top with pastry. Bake at 350 degrees for 1 hour or until crust is brown.

Alabama Cooperative Extension Service, Auburn University

Dove Casserole No. 1

8 dove breasts
1 medium onion, minced
2 tablespoons margarine
Garlic salt, to taste
1 bay leaf
Rosemary, to taste
1 cup white wine
1 cup water
2 cups whipping cream
Salt and pepper, to taste
1/4 bell pepper, minced

Saute margarine, onion, garlic, bay leaf, rosemary and bell pepper in skillet until onion is clear. Add doves and saute until brown. Add wine and water. Cover and simmer for 30 minutes. Remove dove and bay leaf. Strain pan juices into a 2-quart casserole dish. Add cream slowly while stirring. Add salt. Put doves in casserole dish, cover and heat to boiling. Serve hot.

Alabama's Wild Game

Dove Casserole No. 2

15 dove breasts
2 large onions, chopped
1/2 pound mushrooms, chopped
1 stick margarine
Parsley to taste
Garlic salt to taste
2 cans whole tomatos, with juice
2 stalks celery, chopped
1 teaspoon thyme
1/2 teaspoon basil
Salt and pepper, to taste.

Saute onions, mushrooms, parsley and celery. Add doves and brown on both sides. Place mixture and doves in casserole dish and add remaining ingredients. Stir. Bake at 350 degrees for 2 hours.

Dove Stew

4 dove breasts per person
Buttermilk
Flour
1/2 cup margarine
1 small onion, minced
1 teaspoon seasoned salt
1/4 teaspoon thyme
1/4 teaspoon white pepper
Water
Burgundy wine (optional)
Hot cooked rice

Puncture dove breasts and soak in overnight in buttermilk. Drain and dry thoroughly. Coat breasts with flour. Fry in margarine. Add onion, salt, thyme and pepper; cover with water. Cover the pan and simmer until tender, about 30 to 45 minutes. Add wine. If necessary, thicken sauce with flour. Serve over rice.

Alabama Cooperative Extension Service, Auburn University

Alabama's Wild Game

Dove Supreme

12 dove breasts
Flour
Vegetable oil
2 cans beef consomme
1 carrot, chopped fine
3 stalks celery, chopped fine
1 medium onion, chopped fine
1/4 cup cooking sherry
1/4 cup flour
Hot cooked brown rice
1/2 pound mushrooms, chopped

Flour dove and brown in hot oil. Drain well. Place in 2-quart casserole dish. Pour consomme in saucepan. Stir in carrot, celery, onion and sherry. Heat. Thicken with flour to the consistency of gravy, but avoid getting too thick. Pour gravy over doves. Cover casserole. Heat in 325-degree oven for 1 hour. Serve with brown rice and sauteed mushrooms.

Alabama Cooperative Extension Service, Auburn University

Alabama's Wild Game

Dressing dove

The dove is a smallish bird and you are wasting your time if you try to save anything but the breast. Unlike a quail breast which is quite large and has white meat, a dove breast is rather small and has a darker, richer meat.

Start the dressing process (diagram 1) by plucking the feathers on the front of the bird from under the throat to the anus. Pinch the skin near the anus and tear it upwards toward the throat, exposing the breast. Place the thumb under the breast and pull it upward with a steady motion until you hear a pop. This is the wing bones breaking. Use an old pair of scissors to clip the wing bones and neck bone and remove the breasts.

Wash each breast in cold, running water. Study each breast carefully, using a pair of tweezers to remove bird shot and feathers driven into the breast by the bird shot. The feathers will give the meat a strong taste if not removed.

Breasts may be cooked whole in most recipes, but the meat should be cut away (diagram 2) for stir fry and shish kebobs. Use a filet knife to gently cut along the dotted lines to remove the meat.

Alabama's Wild Game

Mourning dove

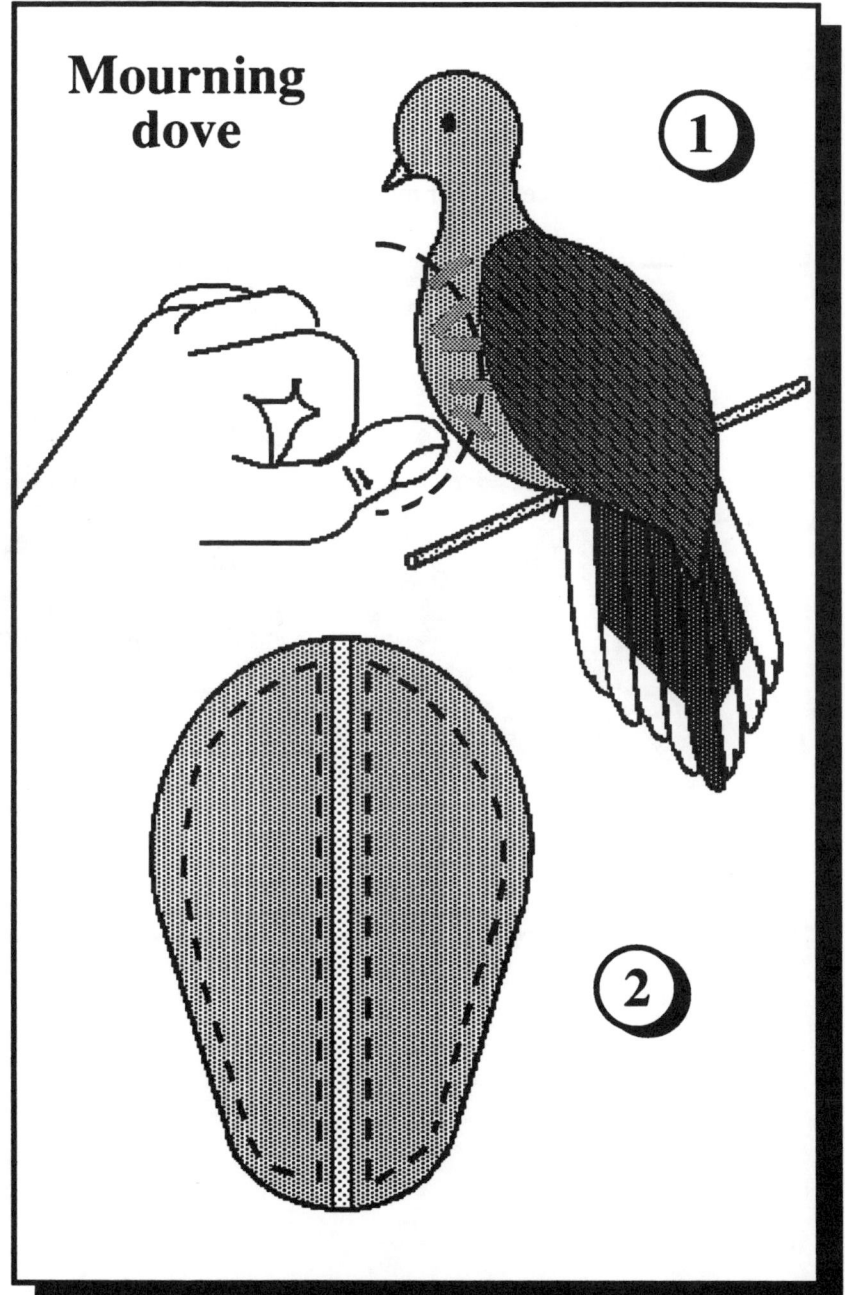

Alabama's Wild Game _____

Alabama's Wild Game

Duck

Being on the eastern border of the central flyway, Alabama gets enough migratory waterfowl every winter to offer some decent duck hunting. Alabama's duck hunting is by no means the quality of that found in Texas, Louisiana, Arkansas or even Mississippi, but when the limit is three birds per day per person, this state's winter population surely qualifies as adequate.

When you say the Tennessee Valley offers the state's best duck hunting, you'll get no arguments from hunters. The Tennessee River lakes of Guntersville, Wheeler, Wilson and Pickwick are unquestionably the top duck hunting spots in the state. Besides offering the most numbers, these lakes also offer the most species.

The Mobile Delta, which is out of driving distance for most Alabama duck hunters, offers some good hunting. The Tenn-Tom Waterway, the Tombigbee River and it's tributaries offer good hunting for West Alabama duck callers and the Coosa River impoundments of Weiss, Neely Henry, Logan Martin and Lay offer fair hunting.

Although duck hunting is steeped in tradition and duck recipes are passed from generation to generation, I've found duck to be the Alabama game species people like the least.

Wild duck meat is darker and dryer than the meat found on commercially raised ducks and it has an almost bloody taste. Because of its dryness, it can't stand much cooking and is

Alabama's Wild Game

usually served rare.

It's much easier to skin a duck than plucking it, but the skin holds in an underlayer of fat that helps keep the meat moist when cooking. To help retain or add moisture, it's not a bad idea to roast ducks with strips of bacon draped across the breast.

Coots, which are technically rails, not ducks, are best skinned, however, for their skin gives the unfinished product an unpleasant taste.

Duck recipes

Roast Duck With Wild Rice Dressing

1 duck
Giblets
1 cup wild rice
4 tablespoons margarine
Salt
Black pepper
Seasoning salt
2-ounce jar pimentos
2-ounce can mushrooms
2 tablespoons chopped green pepper
1 celery stalk, chopped
1 medium onion, chopped
1/4 cup chicken broth
1 apple
4 strips bacon

Soak dressed whole duck in salted icewater overnight. Cook giblets in chicken broth until tender. Cook rice in 1 quart of boiling water; drain. Melt margarine in large skillet and add all ingredients, including giblets. Simmer 5 minutes. Remove duck from salt water and wipe bird dry. Salt body cavity and stuff 1/4 apple into neck of cavity. Stuff cavity lightly with dressing. Lay bacon strips across breasts. Wrap bird in aluminum foil and and bake at 325 degrees for 3 hours.

Alabama's Wild Game

Barbecued Mallard on the Grill

1 mallard, dressed
1/2 cup salad oil
1/4 cup lemon juice
2 cups barbecue sauce of choice

Mix salad oil and lemon juice and brush on duck inside and out. Pour 1/4 cup of barbecue sauce in cavity and brush throughout. Brush remaining barbecue sauce on outside of bird. Place bird in foil-lined bread pan and place on the grill. Cook over slow coals until done throughout. Check for doneness with fork.

Mike and Beth Bolton

Roast Duck

1 duck, dressed
2 apples
1 orange, sliced
1 12-ounce jar sweet and sour sauce

Soak duck overnight in chilled salt water. Boil 20 minutes in salt water. Peel apples and chop. Stuff body cavity with chopped apples. Place orange slices on breast and hold with toothpicks. Cover duck with sweet and sour sauce. Wrap in aluminum foil and bake at 275 degrees for 3 hours.

Alabama's Wild Game

Dressing ducks

Start by plucking all of the feathers. If you have just a few ducks, it's quicker to do this by hand. If you have numbers of ducks, plucking is done best by dipping the whole duck in a large paraffin pot. To make a paraffin pot, melt 1 pound of wax in 6 quarts of boiling water. Remove the pot from the heat source and dip the whole bird in the mixture. Allow the wax to harden and when you peel away the wax, the feathers come off too. It's not necessary to remove the wing feathers since the wings will be cut off.

After the feathers are removed, start by cutting the head off (diagram 1, cut No. 1). Using a sharp knife, make a cut (cut No. 2) from the anus to the throat, being careful not to rupture the intestines. Remove all the insides with your hands. Cut off the wings (cut No. 3) and the legs (cut. No. 4).

You will likely now notice that tiny feathers, called pin feathers, are still on the bird (diagram 2). These may be singed away with a match, or may be pulled off with a piece of folded masking tape (sticky side up). Check the bird for shot holes and remove any pellets and imbedded feathers with a pair of tweezers. Cut away any bloodshot meat.

Alabama's Wild Game

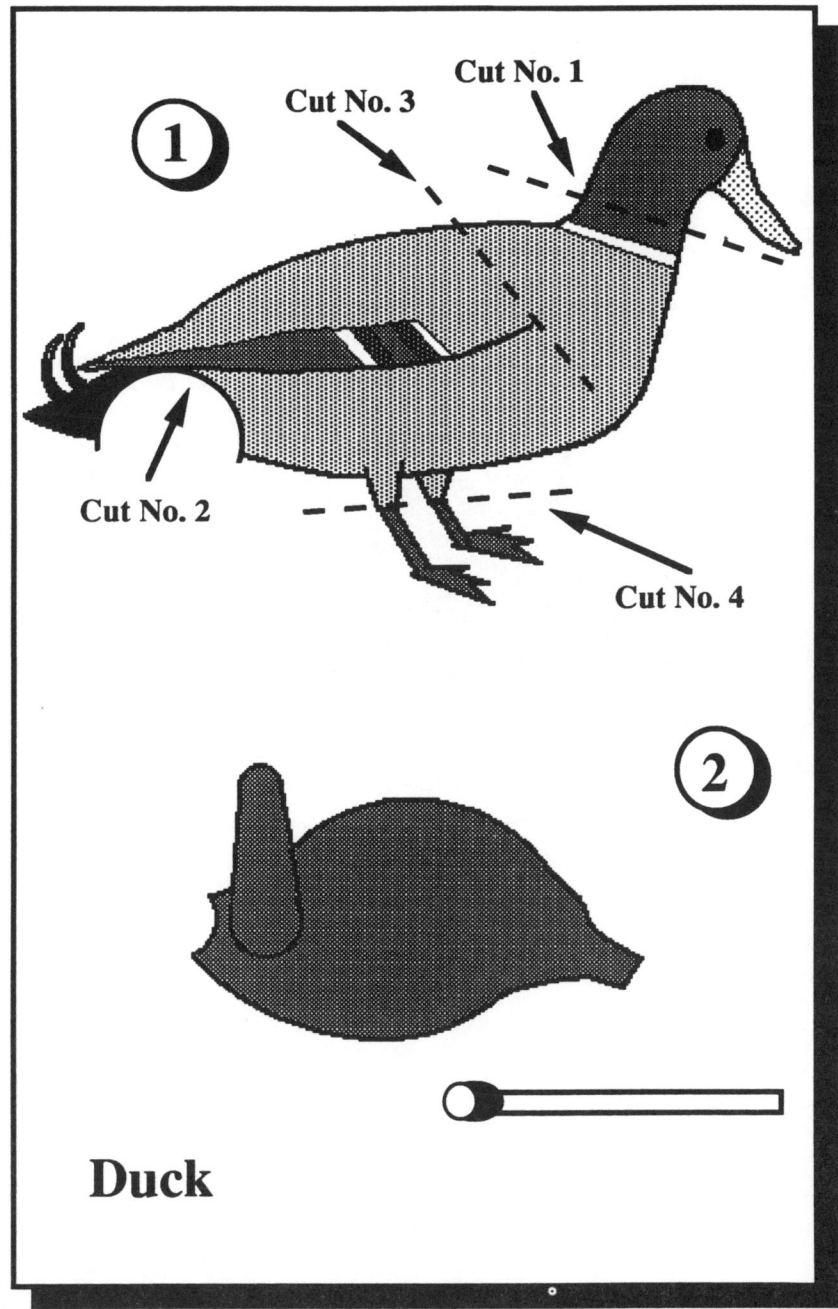

Duck

Alabama's Wild Game

Frog legs

The Alabama outdoorsman who has never been frog gigging cannot lay claim to being a real outdoorsman. Anyone can sit in a tree and shoot deer. It takes a real man to get into an aluminum boat on a sweltering summer night and swat mosquitos on a lake infested with water moccasins and alligators.

Some of my memorable moments in Alabama's great outdoors have come while frog gigging. Getting dumped in slime-filled swamps and accidently gigging snakes is - believe it or not - fun. Keep in mind that it is the kind of fun that matures only several years after the fact, however.

Of all the game-harvesting endeavors in Alabama, frog gigging is the least expensive and easiest to learn. All that is needed is an old aluminum boat (you can wade if you don't have a boat, or if you're a fool), a frog gig (about $3), a cane pole to attach it to (about $2), a flashlight (about $5) and pillow case (free, if you're wife or mamma ain't looking).

Frog gigging is best in late spring and summer when the throaty creatures are voicing their presence with their unmistakable melody. This makes finding a good frog-gigging hole rather easy. Frogs are a nasty bunch and the swampier and nastier the water, the better. All one must do is paddle quietly around the bank of a swamp, lake or pond shining a flashlight in the weeds in search of a pair of glowing eyes. A well-placed shot with the gig between those eyes will result in a flopping

Alabama's Wild Game

mess of swamp creature and more often than not, it will be a frog. It's always best to bring an extra frog gig because if those glowing eyes turn out to be a moccasin, chances are you'll want to donate the original gig to a worthwhile cause, like the bottom of the body of water.

Frog leg recipes

Fried Frog Legs

20 sets frog legs
2 eggs, well beaten
4 cups cracker crumbs
Vegetable oil
Salt and pepper to taste

Salt and pepper frog legs. Dip legs into egg mixture and batter in cracker crumbs. Drop legs in hot oil and brown on both sides. Don't overcook. Guaranteed to make you tap your foot when eating.

Mike and Beth Bolton

Cajun Frog Legs

20 sets frog legs
2 eggs, well beaten
1 cup flour
Vegetable oil
1 large onion, sliced thin
Garlic salt, to taste
1 12-ounce jar piquante sauce
Water

Dip legs in egg mixture, then batter in flour. Pour oil in skillet 1/8-inch deep and fry legs until golden brown. Remove legs and drain on paper towel. Slowly add remaining flour and stir until mixture in lightly brown. Add onion and garlic salt and stir until onion softens. Add piquante sauce and stir until oil rises to top. Add water to desired consistency. Place frog legs in mixture and simmer 10 minutes.

Mike and Beth Bolton

Broiled Frog Legs

20 sets frog legs
1 1/2 cup whole milk
Seasoning salt, to taste
3 sticks margarine
Water

Soak frog legs in milk for at least two hours. Season heavily with seasoning salt. Place legs in baking dish and add sticks of margarine. Place under oven broiler and turn legs frequently and baste. Broil until legs turn brown.

Alabama's Wild Game

Dressing frogs

Alabama frogs rarely grow large, so it takes a few to make a mess. Plan on about 10 sets of frog legs per person. Frog legs have a white meat that is very tasty.

Preparing frog legs to be cooked is one of the easiest dressing chores you'll find in Alabama's outdoors. Start by using a sharp knife or scissors to cut the legs off at the hip joint (diagram No. 1, cuts No. 1 and No. 2). Then, using a sharp filet knife inserted between the skin and meat, cut down the length of the leg (diagram No. 2). You can then use a pair of pliers to pull the skin off just like a glove. Once the skin has been pulled down to the feet, cut the feet off (cuts No. 3 and No. 4). Be sure to wash the legs thoroughly before cooking.

Alabama's Wild Game

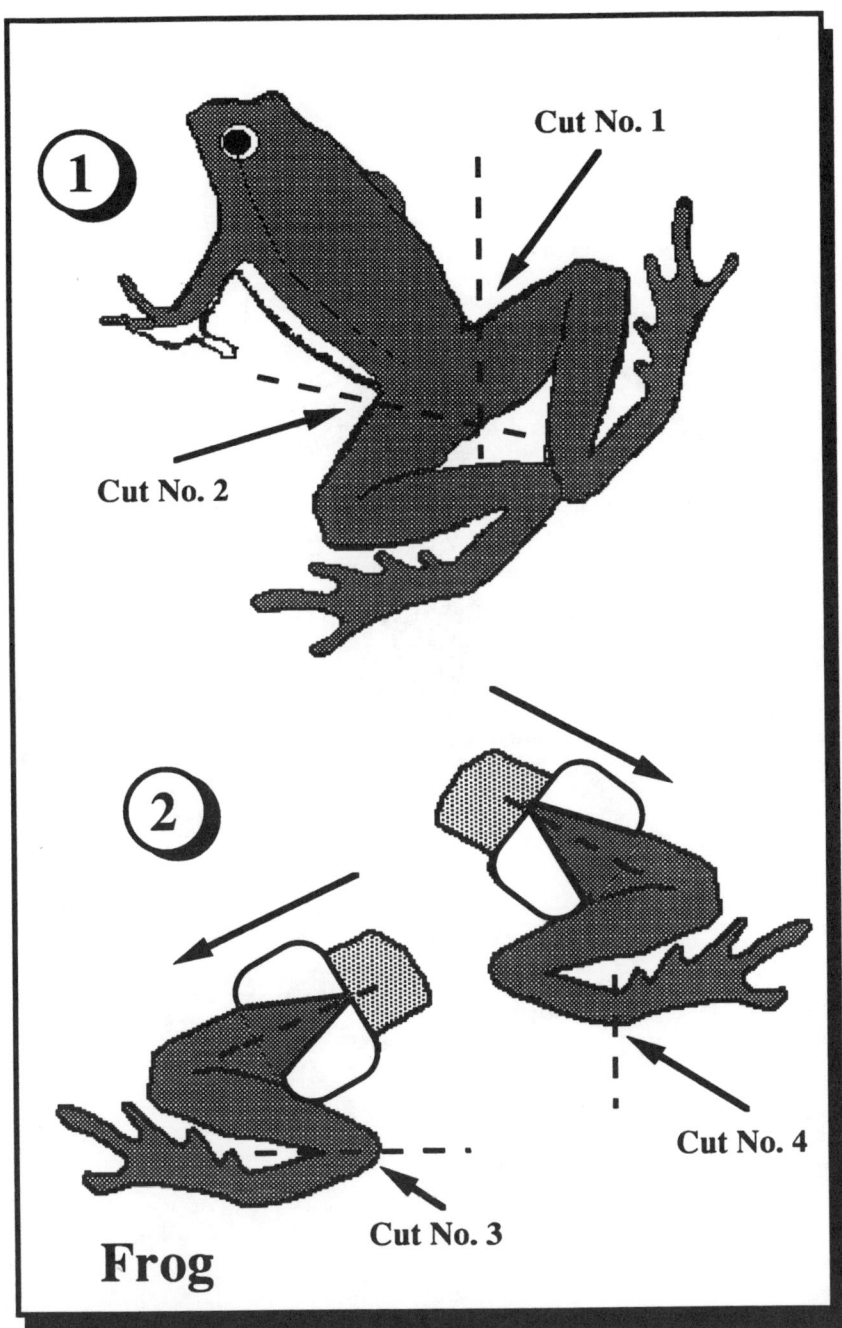

Frog

Alabama's Wild Game _____

Geese

Wild geese aren't that common in Alabama. Since Alabama is on the eastern edge of the Mississippi Flyway, most geese bypass Alabama for Kentucky, Arkansas, Louisiana, Texas and Mississippi.

Large numbers of greater Canada geese winter at Wheeler National Wildlife Refuge near Decatur, and an occasional blue, speckle belly and snow goose appear there. Few of those birds leave the refuge, however. That refuge is not open to hunting.

Wild greater Canada geese appear in small numbers along the Tennessee River. A large number of native Canada geese, most placed by the Tennessee Valley Waterfowl Association, a conservation group intent to returning north Alabama to levels of 50 years ago, are now abundant along the river.

A hunter who is lucky enough to bag a goose species other than a Canada goose has a rare trophy indeed.

Canada geese, geese probably placed by individuals, also have been appearing on the Coosa River on Weiss Lake and Lake Neely Henry in recent years.

A small number of Canada geese also appear every winter at Eufaula National Wildlife Refuge. Limited hunting is allowed on that refuge and waterfowl hunters on Lake Eufaula rarely get a shot at those geese.

Wild goose makes excellent table fare. It's less dark than duck and has an excellent taste. Many prefer goose over duck.

Alabama's Wild Game

Goose recipes

Stuffed Goose

1 Canada goose, dressed with giblets
1 cup hot water
1 box Stovetop Stuffing
1 large onion
Salt and pepper, to taste
Garlic salt, to taste
Water
2 tablespoons margarine
2 apples, diced

Boil giblets in water until tender. Chop fine and add Stovetop Stuffing, onion, apples, salt and pepper and garlic salt. Add water to moisten stuffing. Stuff goose with stuffing and place in roaster. Melt margarine and pour over goose. Cover and roast at 325 degrees until brown.

Fried Canada Goose and Black Wild Rice

1 goose, cut into pieces
Flour
Vegetable oil
Salt and pepper
Pepper Duck (optional)
Water

Salt, pepper and (optional) sprinkle pieces with Pepper Duck, a waterfowl seasoning available at some gourmet outlets. Dredge in flour. Brown goose pieces on both sides. Add 1 cup of water and bring to simmer. Cook 45 minutes, or until meat is tender. Serve on Minnesota-grown black wild rice (also available at gourmet outlets).

Mike Bolton

Potato-Stuffed Canada Goose

1 Canada goose, dressed
3 medium-size potatoes, peeled
1 orange peel, grated
2 tablespoons margarine
2 teaspoons sage
1 small onion, minced
Salt and pepper, to taste
1/2 cup milk

Boil potatoes and mash. Add salt and pepper, to taste. Add grated orange peel, sage, melted margarine, onion and milk. Stuff bird with mixture. Roast at 400 degrees under a loose sheet of foil until done, 1 1/2 to 2 1/2 hours, depending on size. After one hour, baste with drippings. Approximately 30 minutes before end of cooking time, remove foil and allow goose to brown.

Mesquite-Smoked Canada Goose

1 Canada goose
1 cup lemon juice
Garlic salt, to taste
Oregano, to taste
Lemon pepper
Black pepper

Wash goose thoroughly and wipe dry inside and out. Brush whole bird inside and out with lemon juice. With bird still damp from lemon juice, sprinkle liberally with all other ingredients. After coals in smoker have burned down, add mesquite chips and broil goose for three hours over pan of water.

Robert Melvin, Birmingham

Alabama's Wild Game

Canada Goose Stroganoff

2 Canada geese breasts
2 cans Campbell's Cream of Mushroom soup
4 cups of milk
1/2 pound fresh mushrooms, sliced
Vegetable oil
Salt and pepper to taste
Flour

Remove the breasts from two Canada geese and use a filet knife to separate the meat from the breast bone. Cut the breast meat into finger-length strips 1/4-inch thick. Wash breast meat in cold water and shake dry. Heat 1/4-inch vegetable oil in skillet. Sprinkle breast strips lightly with salt and pepper and batter in flour. Cook strips until brown, then place on paper towel to drain. Mix mushroom soup and milk in bowl and blend until smooth. Add this mixture slowly to vegetable oil to make a gravy. Add breast strips and mushrooms and cook 15 minutes over low heat. Feeds 6.

Dressing geese

Start by plucking all of the feathers. If you have just a few geese, it's quicker to do this by hand. If you have numbers of geese, plucking is done best by dipping the whole goose in a large paraffin pot. To make a paraffin pot, melt 1 pound of wax in 6 quarts of boiling water. Remove the pot from the heat source and dip the whole bird in the mixture. Allow the wax to harden and when you peel away the wax, the feathers come off too. It's not necessary to remove the wing feathers since the wings will be cut off.

After the feathers are removed, start by cutting the head off (diagram 1, cut No. 1). Using a sharp knife, make a cut (cut No. 2) from the anus to the throat, being careful not to rupture the intestines. Remove all the insides with your hands. Cut off the wings (cut No. 3) and the legs (cut. No. 4).

You will likely now notice that tiny feathers, called pin feathers, are still on the bird (diagram 2). These may be singed away with a match, or may be pulled off with a piece of folded masking tape (sticky side up). Check the goose for shot holes

Alabama's Wild Game

and remove any pellets and imbedded feathers with a pair of tweezers. Cut away any bloodshot meat.

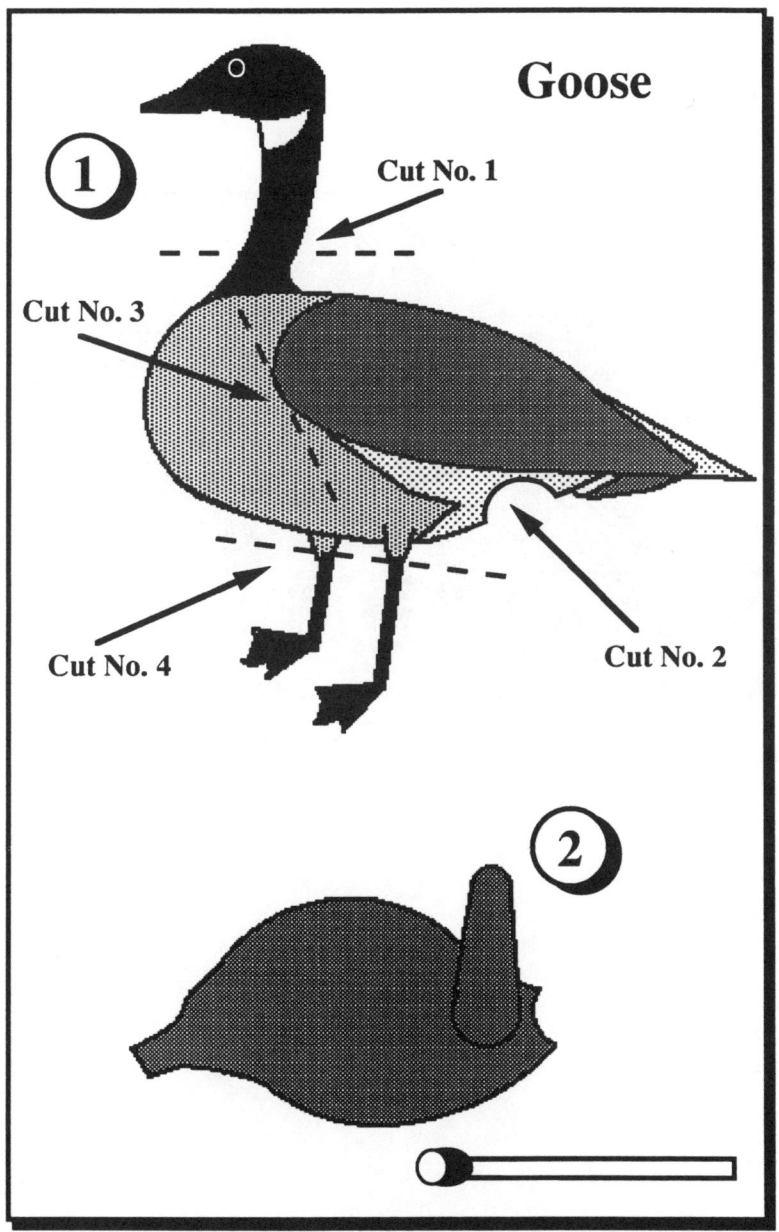

Alabama's Wild Game _____

Muskrat

The muskrat has always been coveted by trappers in Alabama for its luxurious pelt, but because its name contains "rat," Alabamians and others have generally ignored its wonderful, flavorful meat.

Unbeknownst to most, muskrat is grown commercially for its meat in some parts of the country and is sold under a less disgusting name - marsh hare - which fools many into believing they are eating rabbit.

How funny we are about what we eat. Most of think nothing of eating pork, which doesn't mind eating or making a bed out its own excrement, or chicken, which will eat anything that hits the ground. We then cringe at the thought of eating a muskrat, which thoroughly washes itself several times daily with its swims in lakes, rivers and streams and has a diet of nothing but water and shore plants.

The meat of a muskrat is deep red, fine textured, tender and quite good.

Alabama's Wild Game

Muskrat recipes

Barbecued Muskrat

1 muskrat, cut into pieces
3 tablespoons vegetable oil
2 tablespoons white vinegar
2 tablespoons ketchup
1/4 cup lemon juice
1/2 teaspoon salt
1/8 teaspoon black pepper
1/8 teaspoon garlic salt
Cayenne pepper, to taste

Place muskrat pieces in shallow, foil-lined pan. Make sauce from remaining ingredients and brush on pieces. Pour remaining sauce in bottom of pan. Bake uncovered at 300 degrees for 90 minutes or until tender, basting every 15 minutes.

Fried Muskrat

1 muskrat, cut into pieces
1/8 cup Dale's Steak Seasoning
1/8 cup water
1/2 teaspoon salt
1/8 teaspoon black pepper
1/4 cup flour
1/2 egg yolk, beaten
1 cup fine bread crumbs
3 tablespoons vegetable oil

Wash pieces and shake dry. Mix flour, salt and pepper and roll pieces in mixture. Dip in egg mixture and shake dry. Roll in bread crumbs. Drop pieces in hot oil and brown on both sides. Add water and Dale's Steak Seasoning and simmer until meat is done.

Marinated Muskrat

1 muskrat, cut into pieces
1/2 teaspoon salt
Black pepper, to taste
Nutmeg, to taste
6 tablespoons white vinegar
3 tablespoons sugar
3 cups water
2 tablespoons vegetable oil
1 large onion, sliced
1/4 cup chopped green pepper
2 tablespoons chopped celery
1/2 cup raisins
1 tablespoon celery
1/4 cup sour cream
1/2 bay leaf

Rub muskrat pieces with salt, pepper and nutmeg and place in a crock pot or deep roasting pan. Pour two cups of boiling mixture of vinegar, sugar, water and bay leaf over meat and allow to stand for 4 to 8 hours. Remove meat and drain. Save broth. Brown meat in hot vegetable oil until brown. Remove meat to saucepan. Add vegetables to oil and saute, then sprinkle over meat. Bring broth to boil again, then pour over meat. Cover and simmer 1 1/2 hours. Add raisins to liquid in pan and thicken with flour and sour cream mixed to a smooth paste. Pour sauce over meat and serve.

Alabama's Wild Game

Muskrat Smothered in Onions

1 muskrat, cut into pieces
1 1/2 teaspoons salt
1/4 teaspoon Dale's Steak Seasoning
1 cup sour cream
1/2 cup flour
3 tablespoons vegetable oil
3 large onions, sliced
Salt and pepper, to taste

Roll pieces in salt and flour and brown in vegetable oil. Cover pieces with onions slices and add sour cream, Dale's Steak Seasoning and salt and pepper to taste. Cover and simmer for 1 hour.

Baked Muskrat Stuffed With Sweet Taters

1 muskrat cleaned thoroughly, but not cut up
5 large sweet potatoes
4 tablespoons margarine
1 teaspoon dried savory
1 cup chopped celery
4 slices of bacon
Salt and pepper, to taste

Remove skins from sweet potatoes and boil until tender. Mash potatoes and add margarine, salt and pepper to taste, savory and celery. Stuff muskrat with this stuffing. Use a large needle and heavy cord to sew belly up. Flip muskrat on its stomach in roasting pan and place bacon strips on its back. Bake at 375 degrees for approximately 1 hour. Add 1 inch of water to pan after 10 minutes cooking time. Remove bacon and brown the back under the broiler the final few minutes.

Dressing muskrat

Dressing muskrat is similar to dressing its swimming buddy, the beaver. Begin (diagram No. 1) by cutting off the muskrat's tail (cut No. 1) and feet (cuts No. 2 and No. 3). Make a cut from the anus to the throat (cut No. 4), being careful to cut only the

Alabama's Wild Game

pelt and not into the stomach cavity.

Flip the muskrat over (diagram 2), and, using a sharp skinning knife, continue to trim the pelt away from the meat. You may need to flip the muskrat back and forth until the pelt is trimmed completely away from the meat. Once the pelt is all the way off the body and pulled over the head, cut the head off and discard. Cut open the body cavity and remove the insides.

Trim all fat and wash the muskrat thoroughly. Fill a 48-quart ice chest or similar container with water and add 1 box of baking soda, 1 cup of salt and 1 cup of vinegar. Place the muskrat in the solution and soak overnight. Cut the muskrat into cooking-size pieces and he's ready to cook.

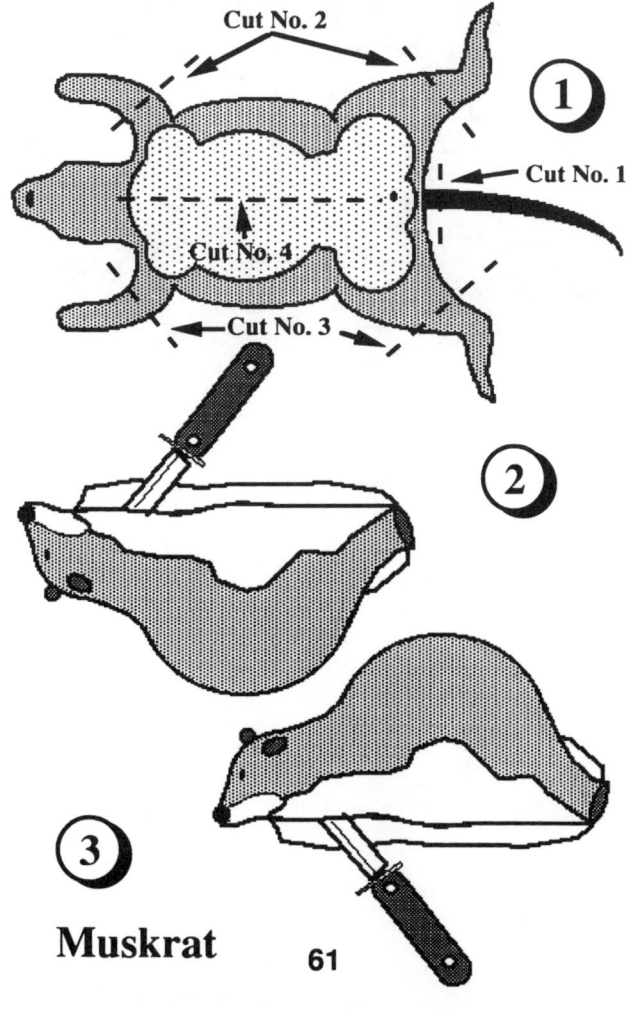

Muskrat

Alabama's Wild Game _____

Alabama's Wild Game

Possum

If you could design the perfect meat, what would it be? A meat that is light in color, fine-grained, tender, low in fat and low in calories would be a good start. How about a meat that doesn't need large pastures to roam or expensive supplemental feed? How about a meat that could be trapped in your backyard, tricked by a few apple slices?

We have just described the possum.

From 1980 to 1984, I lived in Elba, a Coffee County town where possum hunting is a fine art and a good possum hunter demands a certain respect. Starting in October, after farmers harvested their peanut crops, they would often turn their fields over to 'possum hunters to rid them of the hairy little peanut pluckers.

We hunted the peanut fields at night out of an old Ford pickup truck using (I swear this is a true story) my pet greyhound named Megabucks. A peanut-eating possum suddenly caught in the headlights stood no chance against Megabucks. He's leap out of the bed of the truck and bring a squirming, but unharmed, possum back in no time flat.

There's nothing quite like sitting around the camp fire at a good possum barbecue and listening to Farley Taylor of the Taylor-Made Opry on Dothan's WTVY on a crisp October Saturday night in Elba.

If you do not have a greyhound, fret not. There are other tried

Alabama's Wild Game

and true methods of hunting, or trapping, the creature. The easiest way - and keep in mind, possums aren't above visiting the backyards of city folks - is the tried and true tile drain pipe trap.

If you live near woods and have an unfenced yard, get a section of tile drain pipe, dig a hole and bury one end so the pipe slants at a 45° angle and the other end is low enough for the possum to crawl in. Throw a few sliced apples or a handful of peanuts in the hole and the possum will crawl in, but he'll find it too slick to back out. He can be removed by pulling him out by the tail.

Possum recipes

Mike Bolton's Barbecued Possum

1 possum, dressed, but not cut up
1 stick of margarine
2 cups white vinegar
1/2 cup Dale's Steak Seasoning
Barbecue sauce of choice

Turn possum on its back and spread body cavity open. Use a hatchet to split backbone down the middle so possum will spread flat on the grill. Cook possum over medium coals, brushing often with mixture of melted margarine, vinegar, and Dale's. Just before possum is done throughout, brush inside and out with barbecue sauce and cook until barbecue sauce cooks into the meat. Do not burn.

Mike Bolton, Argo

Iron Skillet Fried Possum

3 pounds possum, cut up
3 cups of flour
3 cups bacon grease
Salt and pepper, to taste

Mix flour, salt and pepper in paper bag. Place possum pieces in bag and shake until meat is covered. Remove from bag and

Alabama's Wild Game

pound with a meat hammer. Place back in bag and shake again. Heat grease in heavy iron skillet. Place meat in skillet and cover. Cook until golden brown, turning once. Feeds 6.

Ben D. King, Columbiana

Alabama's Wild Game

Dressing possum

This ain't one of those methods that you ought to call up and describe to the animal rights activists in New York.

Keep in mind that a possum will eat anything - and that includes fingers (just ask Elba's Double Digit Ferguson) - so a well-placed shot to the head with a .22 is a good start.

You'll next need a fire. Most country folks are always burning something in the backyard (usually something with a good aroma, like a steel-belted radial), but if you live in the city, you may have to go out of your way to start a wood fire. Allow the fire to burn down and throw the *dead* possum on the fire and burn all the hair off. Turn him several times and pull him out by the tail.

Cut off the front legs (diagram 1, cuts No. 1 and No. 2). Cut around the rear legs and from one rear leg to the other (cut No. 3). Cut around the anus.

Use a rope attached to the rear legs to hang the animal from a limb. Cut the bone in the tail. Make a cut through the skin, making a circle around the possum beginning just below the tail. Pull the skin down the body and over the head and off the front legs. Cut off the head.

Take the possum down and cut off the rear legs. Split the possum from the neck to the anus and remove the intestines.

NOTE: Be sure to remove the small red scent glands located in the lower back and under each front leg.

For roasting or barbecuing, leave the possum whole. For other recipes, cut the possum into serving-size pieces.

Alabama's Wild Game

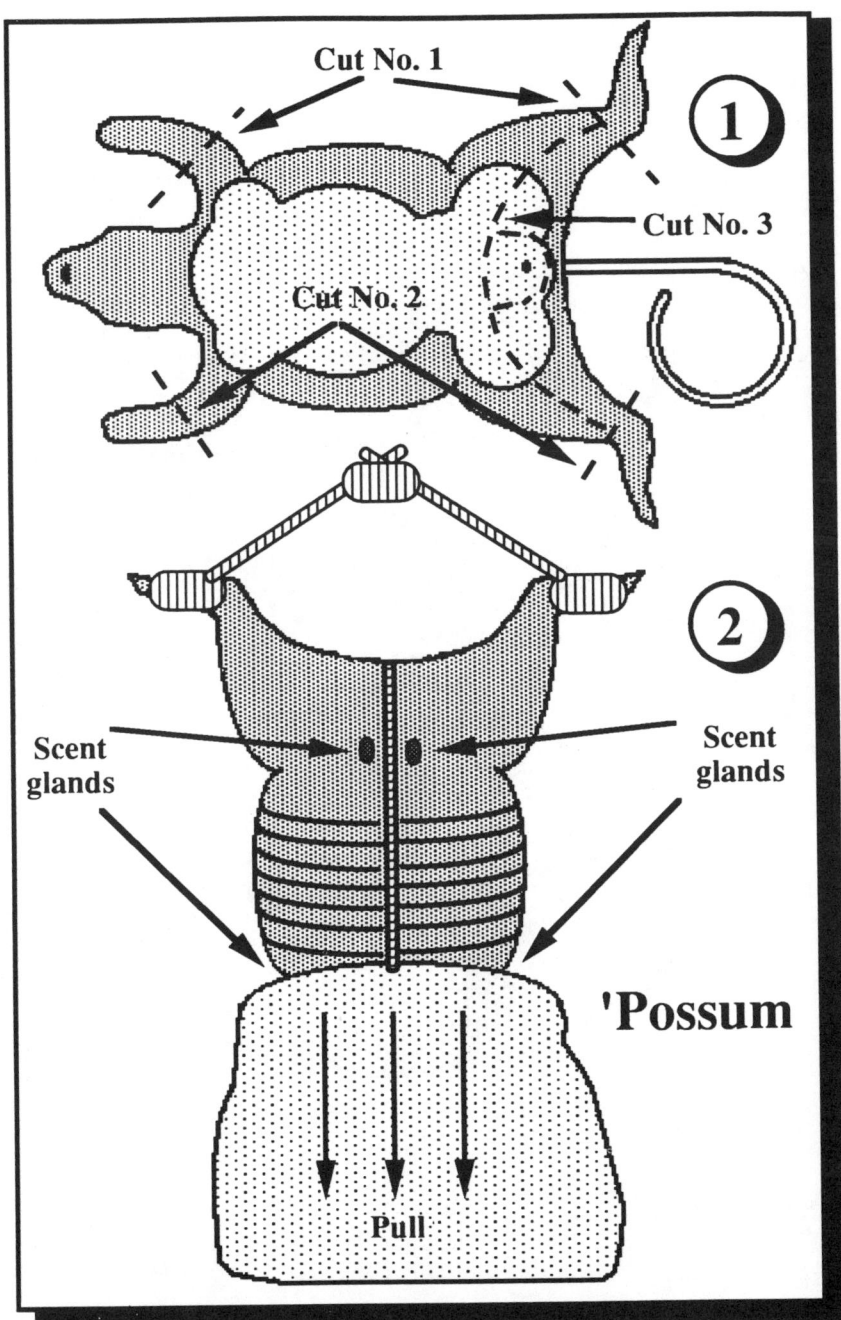

'Possum

Alabama's Wild Game _____

Quail

Only in the past 25 years has the bobwhite quail become a rare sight on the dinner tables in this state. The decline of Alabama's quail population, and the resulting decline in quail hunters, can be attributed to several factors.

When much of the state was in farmland, the untended fence rows and high grasses provided excellent habitat for the bird known for its noisy, often frightening, flushes. Cleaner farming practices, such as Bush Hogging and controlled burning, has caused a rapid decline in that habitat. The loss of cover has made the quail easy prey for hawks, coyotes and wild dogs. The use of pesticides has added to the decline.

Access to quail hunting land also has diminished. Much of the state's prime quail hunting land has been lost to development, converted to pine forests or leased to private clubs or individuals for deer hunting.

Fortunate is the individual who has access to good quail hunting in Alabama these days. It's sad so few have access to quail hunting, because besides being an exciting sport, quail is one of Alabama's true native delicacies.

The uninformed will tell you that quail tastes like chicken, but the uninformed think everything tastes like chicken. Chickens stay up at night praying that they'll someday taste like quail. Quail is a treat with a unique flavor. It's almost foolish to attempt any cooking method that will hide that flavor.

Alabama's Wild Game

Quail are naturally dry, so cook them with steam, or immerse them in liquids whenever possible. This seals in the natural juices and keeps the birds moist. Baste quail often with broth or butter.

Quail are generally small, so they cook quickly in comparison to other meats. Don't overcook.

Quail recipes

Champagne Quail

You can tell your dinner guests that this elegant recipe is a favorite of Queen Elizabeth and she often has her personal chef prepare it with the quail harvested by Prince Charles on his many hunting excursions. That ain't the truth, but your guests will be feeling so good after drinking the leftover champagne, you'll have 'em believing you taught Chuck to shoot.

8 whole quail
1/4 stick of butter
1 1/4 cups champagne
2/3 cup chicken broth

Preheat oven to 325 degrees. Place a colander in a large saucepan and fill saucepan with water 1 inch below colander. Bring to a boil. This is your steamer. Salt and pepper quail and dip into melted butter, covering each bird thoroughly. Drop buttered birds in colander and steam 15 minutes. Move birds to a covered oven-proof dish and pour in champagne and broth. Cook 15 minutes, basting twice. Serve hot. Serves 4.

Beth Bolton

Gene Stallings' Smothered Quail

6 quail, dressed
6 tablespoons butter
3 tablespoons flour
2 cups chicken broth
1/2 cup sherry
Salt and pepper to taste

Alabama's Wild Game

1 can (3 ounce) chopped mushrooms
1 jar apricot preserves
1 box (6 ounce) Uncle Ben's long grain wild rice

Brown quail in butter. Remove to baking dish. Add flour to butter. Stir well. Slowly add broth, sherry and seasonings. Blend thoroughly. Add mushrooms. Pour over quail. Put 1/2 jar of preserves on breasts of the quail. Cover and bake at 350 degrees for one hour. During the last 15 minutes spread remaining preserves over birds. Serve over rice.

Gene Stallings, head football coach, University of Alabama.

Roast Quail With Mushrooms

4 quail, dressed and cleaned
4 bacon slices
1 tablespoon butter or margarine
1/2 cup hot water
Juice of half lemon
1 3-ounce can broiled mushrooms, drained
4 slices toasted bread

Wipe birds inside and out with a clean cloth. Wrap each bird with a slice of bacon and secure with toothpicks. Put birds into a buttered pan and roast at 350 degrees, basting occasionally, about 15-20 minutes, or until tender. Remove birds and add butter, water and lemon juice in pan, stirring to make a gravy. Add mushrooms. Serve the birds on toast with gravy.

Alabama Cooperative Extension Service, Auburn University

Alabama's Wild Game

Easy Baked Quail

Flour
Salt and pepper, to taste
8 quail
Vegetable oil
1 cup of water
Worcestershire sauce
Hot cooked wild or brown rice

Season flour with salt and pepper. Roll quail in seasoned flour and and brown in hot oil. Place birds in a rack in a roasting pan. Add water for steam. Sprinkle birds with worcestershire sauce. Cover with foil and cook at 350 degrees for 30 minutes, or until tender. Make gravy from drippings and serve over rice.

Alabama Cooperative Extension Service, Auburn University

Bacon-Wrapped Quail

8 quail breasts
1/8-inch fatback strips, cut into 2-inch squares
2 sticks of butter or margarine
1/4 cup of lemon juice
Sprinkle of ginger
8 slices of bacon
8 1-inch slices of lemon peel
8 slices of crustless white bread
Ground cinnamon

Heat butter or margarine in deep skillet until it's about to smoke. Quickly brown quail on all sides. Remove birds, but save skillet with butter. Put lemon strip inside of each bird and sprinkle inside with ginger. Spoon lemon juice over each bird and lightly dust each with lemon juice, cinnamon and salt and pepper. Place a fatback square on top of each bird, then wrap with bacon and secure with toothpicks. Return to covered skillet and simmer each bird in butter for 30 minutes, turning birds frequently. Remove birds and increase heat in skillet. Fry bread in remaining stock. Serve birds on fried bread. Be careful not to suck the skin off of your fingers when you're finished eating.

Beth Bolton

Broiled Quail

12 quail
1 teaspoon salt
1/4 teaspoon pepper
6 tablespoons butter, melted

Wipe birds clean with damp cloth. Split the quail, sprinkle with salt and pepper, and rub thoroughly with butter. Place birds skin side down on broiler. Broil for 5 minutes, baste with butter, and broil 5 minutes more. Turn birds, brush with butter, and broil 10 minutes more.
Alabama Cooperative Extension Service, Auburn University

Fireplace Quail

8 quail
2 cups cooked rice
Salt and pepper, to taste
8 thin bacon slices or fatback

Clean, rinse and dry quail. Fill cavities with cooked wild rice. Sprinkle with salt and pepper; wrap each quail with a slice of bacon or salt pork; then wrap each securely in heavy duty aluminum foil. Bury each bird in hot charcoal ashes. Allow birds to roast 30 minutes, then check for tenderness. Be sure to keep wrapped birds covered with hot ashes. Serves 4.

Basic Southern Fried Quail

4 large quail
1/4 cup of flour
1 teaspoon salt
1/8 teaspoon pepper
Vegetable oil

Place flour, salt and pepper in a paper bag. Dip quail in water and shake off excess. Drop quail into bag and shake, covering each bird thoroughly. Heat a frying pan half filled with oil. Brown quail on both sides. Cover skillet and reduce heat. Cook slowly until tender, about 30 minutes, turning once to brown evenly.

Alabama's Wild Game

Mommernims' Quail

This recipe is from New Brockton's Doc Littleton, who says times were so hard during the depression his family couldn't pay attention. He said Sunday dinner always consisted of going to Mommernims to eat quail Paw Paw had shot.

Ever how many quail Paw Paw shot
1 cup chicken broth
4 small wild onions, chopped (one small store-bought onion will do)
1 watercress stalk, chopped (substitute 1 celery stalk)
1 bell pepper, chopped
1 cake of butter (about 1 stick)
1 bacon strip
1 good splash of wine (cooking sherry is better)
2 cups mushrooms
Flour for gravy
Salt and pepper to taste

Melt butter in deep skillet over high heat. Brown quail. Stuff each bird with a mixture of bell peppers, onions and celery. Put birds back in pot and add chicken broth, cooking sherry and other ingredients, except flour. Cover skillet and simmer until tender, about 45 minutes. Remove quail and add mushrooms and flour to skillet to make gravy. Serves 10 no matter how many birds there are.

Deep Fried Quail

This is an excellent recipe for those who have LP fish cookers.

8 quail
Salt and pepper, to taste
1/2 cup of milk
1 egg
Flour
Vegetable oil

Split quail; salt and pepper lightly. Dip each bird into egg and milk mixture. Remove and dust lightly with flour. If using a fish cooker, heat oil until a paper match dropped in the oil lights. If

Alabama's Wild Game

using an electric deep fat fryer or dutch oven, heat oil to 340 degrees. The vegetable oil should just cover the birds. Cook until they are crispy and brown.

Cooperative Extension Service, Auburn University

Quail and Southern Gravy

This recipe provides the 3 basic food groups found in Alabama: Meat, flour and grease. It's guaranteed to make a health nut quit his doctor.

8 quail
Buttermilk
Salt and flour
Vegetable oil
1 tablespoon Dale's steak seasoning

Soak quail in buttermilk for 2 hours. Sprinkle with salt and flour. Brown in deep fat. Drain fat and make flour gravy. Add Dale's to gravy. Place quail in gravy and simmer for 10 minutes.

Guy Hunt's Quail Dumplings

6-8 quail, whole
1/2 stick margarine
1/4 cup vegetable oil
1 1/2 cups self-rising flour
Salt
Water

Place quail in pressure cooker and add just enough water to cover. Adjust pressure cooker to 10 pounds of pressure and cook for 45 minutes. Save broth. Allow quail to cool, then debone. Remove broth to large pan and boil. Add margarine and salt lightly. In a separate bowl, mix mix 1 1/2 cups of flour and vegetable oil. Add just enough water to make oil and flour stick. Mix well. Batter should be stiff. Spoon batter into boiling broth. Keep adding dumplings until there is enough for everyone who plans to eat. Be sure to leave enough juice. Add quail meat and remove from heat. Creating the perfect batter mixture for this recipe takes some experimenting.

Gov. and Mrs. Guy Hunt, Holly Pond

Alabama's Wild Game

Barbecued Quail

8 quail
1 cup finely chopped onion
1/4 cup dark brown sugar
1/4 cup white vinegar
1/4 cup Dale's steak seasoning
1 teaspoon dry mustard
1/4 teaspoon Durkee's red hot pepper sauce
1/2 cup catsup
3 tablespoons vegetable oil

Combine onions, sugar, vinegar, Dale's, mustard, pepper sauce and catsup in a saucepan. Bring to boil over high heat. Reduce to low and simmer uncovered 5-8 minutes, until onions are soft. Heat the oil over high heat (but not smoking) add the quail and fry until brown, about 2-3 minutes on each side. Drain the oil from the skillet. Pour the barbecue sauce over the quail and cover skillet. Simmer over low heat for 15-20 minutes, spooning the sauce over the birds frequently.

Dressing quail

Start by plucking all the quail's feathers, then use a sharp knife to cut off the head (diagram No. 1, cut No. 1). Cut off the legs (cut No. 2) and the wings (cut No. 3). Cut around the anus (cut No. 4) and up to the neck. Remove the insides. Wash the entire bird thoroughly.

Some prefer to use the whole bird in recipes (diagram 2), while others remove the breast (diagram 3) for recipes and save the legs for hors d' oeuvres.

Alabama's Wild Game

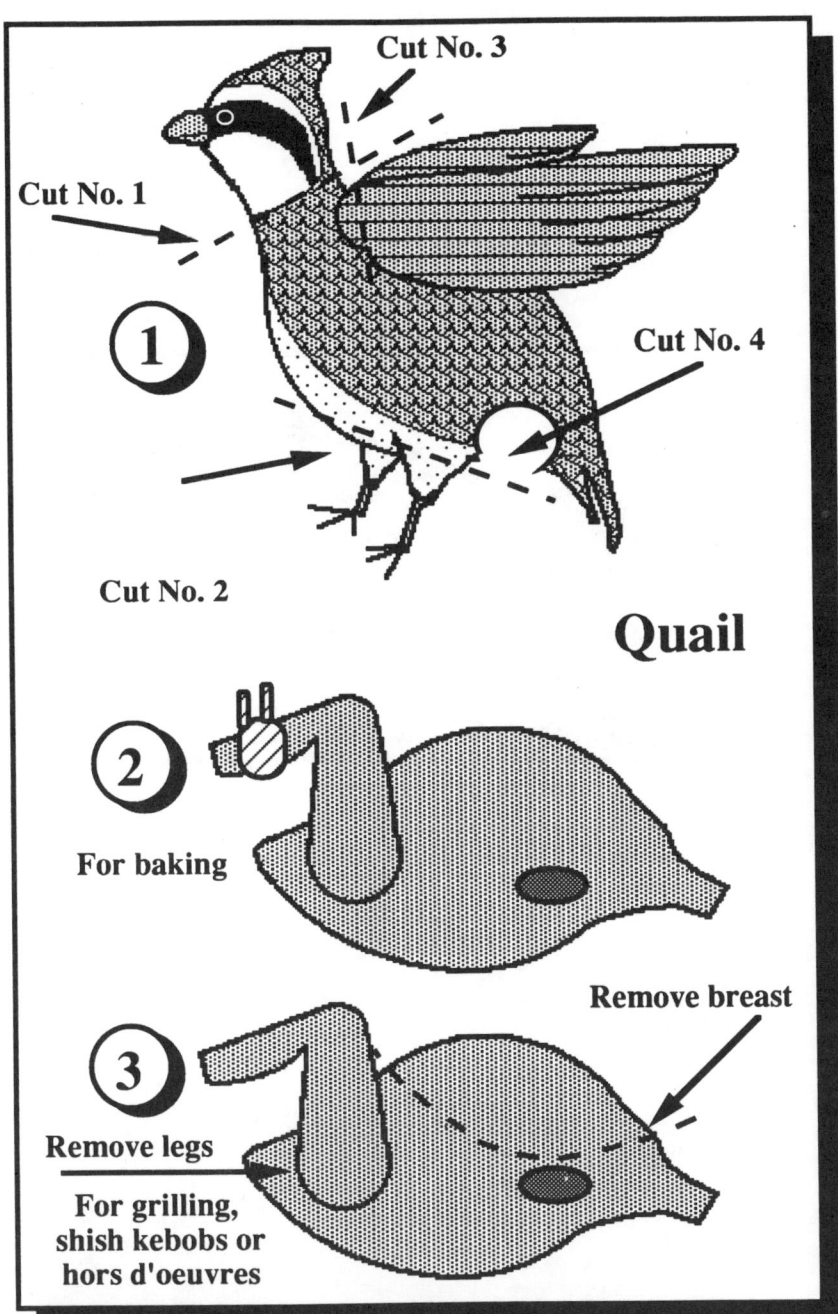

Alabama's Wild Game

Alabama's Wild Game

Rabbit

Chances are that your grandfather or great-grandfather never had the opportunity to fire a shot at a deer or wild turkey, but rather spent many hours on the heels of yelping beagles as they chased cottontails through the briars and brambles.

Before the whitetail deer became king, rabbit hunting was the No. 2 hunted game species (behind squirrel) in Alabama. The number of rabbit hunters in the state has fallen dramatically since 1965 and the downward spiral likely will continue. There are many reasons as to why.

The availability of hunting land is one reason. Most decent land in the state is now used for deer hunting, and deer hunters have no desire to share it with packs of rabbit dogs during the deer season, which overlaps with rabbit season.

Cleaner farming practices such as bush-hogging fence rows has wiped out much of the prime rabbit habitat, also. The rabbit has more enemies now than before, too. Coyotes and hawks find rabbits to be one of their favorite foods. Last, but not least, the cost of maintaining a quality of pack of beagles today is an expense many find to be overwhelming.

Alabama still has its share of rabbit hunters, however, and rabbit is still as good eating as it was when your grandfather put it on his plate.

Rabbits have a pink, delicious meat that almost no one finds objectionable. Young rabbits are unbelievably tender and are good in all recipes. Older, larger rabbits are sometimes tough, and are best when their meat is roughed up with a meat hammer or used in soups, sausages and stews.

Rabbit meat is low in moisture, so don't overcook.

Rabbit recipes

Basic Fried Rabbit

1 rabbit, cut up
1 egg, beaten
1/2 cup milk
1/2 box saltine crackers
Salt and pepper, to taste
Vegetable oil

Place crackers in plastic bag and crush. Mix beaten egg and milk in bowl. Salt and pepper rabbit pieces. Dip pieces in egg and milk mixture and roll in cracker crumbs. Place in hot oil and cook quickly. Turn over each piece once.

Doug and Mary Paramore, New Brockton

Oven Baked Rabbit

1 rabbit, cut up
1/4 cup margarine
1/3 cup Italian bread crumbs
1/2 teaspoon ground rosemary
1/2 teaspoon dry mustard
1/2 cup orange juice
1 tablespoon parsley flakes
Salt and pepper, to taste

Salt and pepper rabbit pieces. Melt margarine in baking dish. Mix all ingredients, except bread crumbs and orange juice, in paper bag. Dip rabbit pieces in margarine and place in bag and shake. Add orange juice to margarine in baking dish and mix well. Arrange rabbit pieces in cooking dish and cover with foil. Bake at 350 degrees for 45 minutes, turn rabbit over and bake another 45 minutes. Place under broiler for 5 minutes with foil removed to brown.

Shake and Bake Rabbit

2 young rabbits, cut up
1 box chicken Shake and Bake

Wash rabbit thoroughly. Place Shake and Bake mixture in plastic bag. Add rabbit pieces one at a time and shake. Place on aluminum-foil lined cookie sheet and follow cooking directions on box.

Grilled Rabbit

1 rabbit, cut up
1/2 cup olive oil
2 tablespoons Dale's Steak Seasoning
1 tablespoon lemon juice
1 teaspoon mustard
1 tablespoon parsley
1 lemon, sliced
Salt and pepper, to taste

Soak rabbit pieces in salty water for one hour. Score the pieces with a sharp knife like a catfish. Brush all pieces with olive oil. Make a sauce by mixing and heating Dale's, lemon juice, mustard and salt and pepper. Grill 20-25 minutes, basting often with sauce. Remove and garnish with parsley and lemon slices.

Broiled Rabbit

2 rabbits, cut up
2 sticks margarine
bacon slices
salt and pepper

Wrap pieces with bacon slices and secure with toothpick. Melt margarine and pour into baking dish. Add rabbit pieces to dish and salt and pepper to taste. Bake at 350 degrees for 45 minutes, basting often with margarine.

Alabama's Wild Game

Rabbit Supreme

2 rabbits, cut up
1/4 cup vinegar
1/4 cup vegetable oil
2 cups flour
1 large onion, sliced thin
Paprika
5 bay leaves
12 peppercorns
1 cup red wine

Soak rabbit overnight in vinegar and salt water. Place flour in sack and add rabbit pieces. Shake well. Remove and sprinkle with paprika. Heat oil in skillet and fry rabbit until golden brown. Place pieces in bottom of baking dish. Place sauteed onion slice on top of each piece. Place half of bay leave on each onion and sprinkle a few peppercorns on each piece. Add water to barely cover meat. Bake at 350 degrees for one hour. Add wine after 30 minutes.

Rabbit Sausage

1 pound rabbit meat (no bones)
1/3 pound bacon ends
1/4 cup onions, minced
Salt and pepper, to taste
Oregano, to taste

Grind both meats through sausage grinder. Mix thoroughly in large bowl and season to taste. Add onions and knead by hand. Make into patties and fry.

Royal Rabbit

1 rabbit, deboned
1 bottle white vinegar
1 medium onion, chopped
12 peppercorns
2 bay leaves
3 tablespoons vegetable oil
1 cup sour cream

Alabama's Wild Game

Salt and pepper, to taste
2 cups flour

Cut deboned rabbit into small pieces and place in jar. Cover with mixture of half vinegar, half water. Add peppercorns, bay leaves, onion and salt and pepper. Place lid on jar and place in refrigerator for at least two days, no more than four. Remove meat and save liquid. Salt and pepper rabbit and roll in flour. Brown on all sides in hot oil. Add 1/4 inch of vinegar mixture. Cover and simmer 1 hour. Remove rabbit, add flour to mixture to make gravy. Add sour cream to gravy and pour over rabbit.

Alabama's Wild Game

Dressing rabbit

Rabbit is one the few game animals in Alabama that you have to be careful of. It sometimes carries a disease called tularemia, or "rabbit fever," which can be serious to humans. Avoid bringing home rabbits that appear tame or behave strangely.

Wear rubber gloves when dressing rabbits and afterwards wash your hands and knife carefully. Once the rabbit is properly cooked, the danger is over.

Start dressing by cutting off the head (diagram No. 1, cut No. 1) and the feet (cuts No. 2 and No. 3). Make a circle cut clear around the rabbit's mid-section without cutting into the meat or internal organs (diagram No. 2) and pull the hide off both ends (diagram No. 3). Cut the rabbit into quarters (diagram No. 4) for most recipes.

Alabama's Wild Game

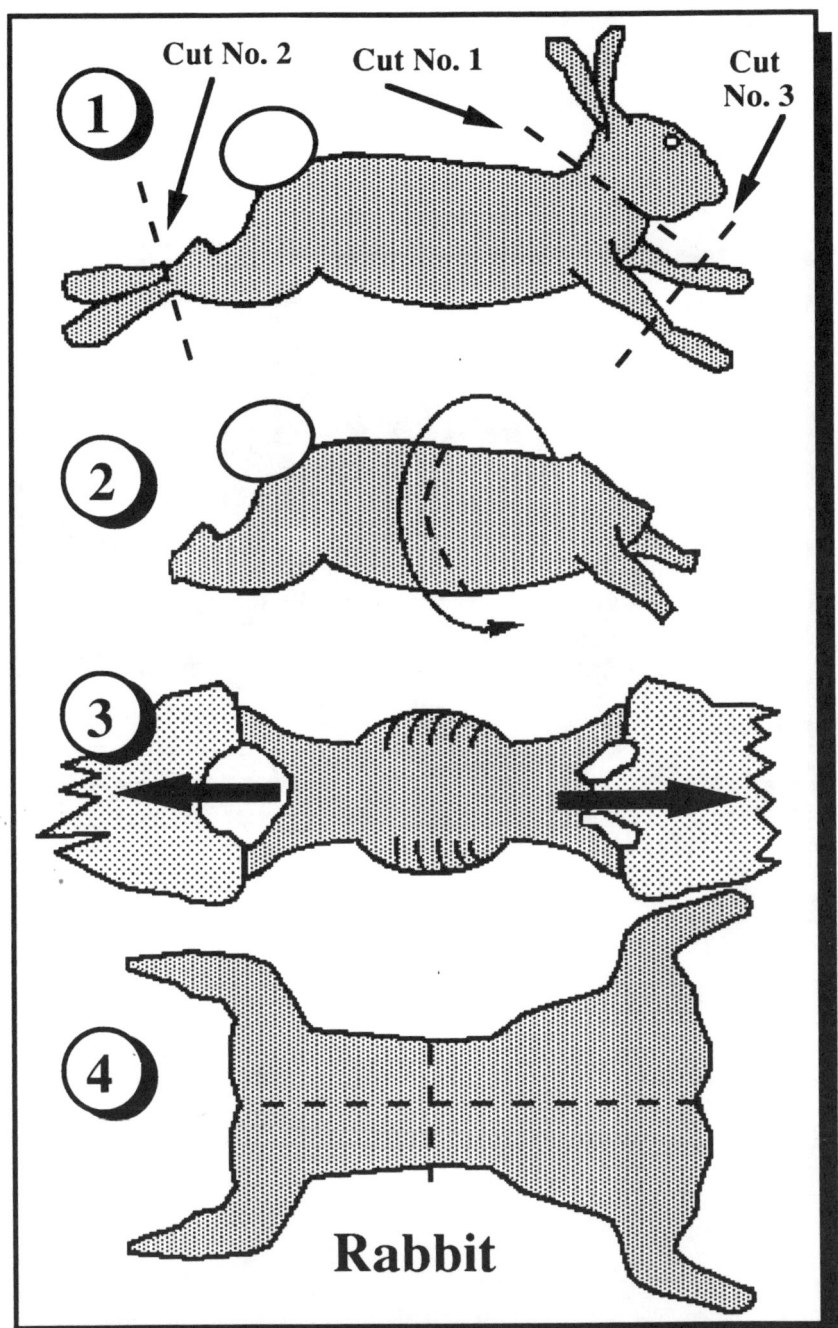

Rabbit

Alabama's Wild Game

Raccoon

'Coon hunting is a tremendously big sport in Alabama, but a sport many aren't aware exists because it's played in the woods at night when most normal human beings are sleeping. For many, its only tell-tale signs are the sleepy co-worker with an empty dog box in the back of his truck.

'Coon hunters are undoubtedly hunting's most dedicated participants. 'Coon hunting trips seem to take place only when it's too hot or too cold and result in forays across chest-high raging creeks in December, up mountains the size of Everest on humid, unseasonably hot nights and hours of looking for lost dogs.

During 'coon season, it's not uncommon for Alabama's woods to be full of yelping dogs and 'coon hunters. Most 'coon hunters aren't hunters in the traditional sense of the word. They enjoy the competition of their dogs chasing and treeing the coon, but rarely do they kill the object of their chase. Most leave the 'coon alive to be chased on another day. 'Coon hunters may be the ultimate hunting conservationists.

Raccoons are amazingly good table fare, however. 'Coons have a meat with texture much like that of the squirrel, only the meat is darker and more tender. An adult 'coon has a surprising amount of edible meat, too. A single 'coon will easily feed four people.

Alabama's Wild Game

Raccoon recipes

Baked Raccoon

1 raccoon, cut into pieces
2 strips salt pork, or "fatback"
Seasoning salt
2 bay leaves
1 cup Dale's Steak Seasoning
Water

Place raccoon pieces in roaster and add water to cover pieces. Add Dale's Steak Seasoning. Parboil raccoon pieces for 15 minutes, or until tender. Remove pieces and save broth. Sprinkle pieces with seasoning salt. Place a piece of salt pork on top of each piece and pin with toothpick. Move pieces to baking dish and pour broth over each piece. Bake at 325 degres for 90 minutes, basting occasionally with broth.

Old Fashioned Baked Coon

1 coon, cut into pieces
5 sweet potatoes
1 cup chicken broth
1 teaspoon sage
Salt and pepper, to taste

Parboil raccoon pieces until tender. Place in baking dish and sprinkle with sage and salt and pepper. Add broth. Precook sweet potatoes, cut in half and place around the raccoon. Bake in 425 degree oven for 20 minutes.

Coon and Dressing

1 raccoon, cut into pieces
Salt and pepper
10 slices white bread
2 eggs, well beaten
2 tablespoons sage
1/2 teaspoon ground clove
1 cup chicken broth

Salt and pepper raccoon pieces. Cook in pressure cooker for 1 hour at 15 pounds of pressure, or parboil if raccoon is young. Make dressing by soaking cut up bread pieces in broth and adding beaten eggs, sage and ground clove. Arrange pieces in baking dish and cover with dressing. Bake at 350 degrees until dressing is browned.

Barbecued Raccoon

1 raccoon, cut into pieces
6 carrots, sliced
3 onions, chopped
1/2 teaspoon ground sage
Garlic salt, to taste
Salt and pepper, to taste
2 bay leaves
Water
1/2 gallon barbecue sauce

Mix all above ingredients, except barbecue sauce, and add raccoon pieces. Simmer 2 hours. Save broth. Remove raccoon meat from bone and place meat in Dutch oven. Add 1 cup of broth and barbecue sauce. Simmer for 1 hour. Make gravy for potatoes from the remaining broth.

Fricasseed Raccoon

1 raccoon, cut into pieces
2 tablespoons Dale's Steak Seasoning
Salt and pepper, to taste
Flour
Vegetable oil
2 cups beef broth

Salt and pepper raccoon pieces and powder with flour. Fry in 1/2 inch of vegetable oil until brown. Add Dale's Steak Seasoning and broth to skillet. Cover and simmer for two hours.

Alabama's Wild Game

Raccoon Meat Loaf

1 raccoon, cut into pieces and deboned
1/2 cup bread crumbs
1/2 tablespoon onion salt
1/2 tablespoon garlic salt
1 tablespoon salt
1 tablespoon pepper
2 eggs, well beaten
1/4 teaspoon thyme
1 cup evaporated milk

Cut meat off of bones and run through a sausage grinder. Mix ground meat with bread crumbs, onion salt, garlic salt, salt, pepper, beaten eggs, evaporated milk and thyme. Mix well. Form into a roll and place in deep pan. Bake in 350 degrees oven for 90 minutes.

Raccoon Goulash

1 raccoon, deboned and cubed
1 pound fresh okra, sliced
3 cups beef broth
1 tablespoons garlic salt
1 teaspoon ground cloves
2 bay leaves
1 teaspoon salt
1/4 teaspoon black pepper
3 tablespoons margarine
3 tablespoons flour
2 tablespoons paprika
1 can stewed tomatoes
Vegetable oil

Brown raccoon cubes in hot oil. Remove meat and drain on paper towel. Move meat to large soup pot. Add broth, garlic salt, bay leaves, salt, black pepper and okra. Simmer 2 1/2 hours. Withdraw 1 cup of mixture. Cream butter, flour and paprika and add to cup of mixture; mix well, and return to soup pot. Simmer until goulash thickens. Add tomatoes and simmer 15 more minutes.

Alabama's Wild Game

How wild game compares

Here's how some of Alabama's most popular wild game compares nutrition-wise with other commonly eaten meat. Comparisons are based on 100 grams, edible portion. (Approximately 3.6 ounces):

Food description	Water (percent)	Calories	Protein (percent)	Fat (percent)
Beef: choice grade, trimmed, raw	51.7	356	16.3	31.6
Pork: composite of trimmed, lean meat, medium fat class, raw	45.5	384	23.6	31.4
Lamb: choice grade, trimmed, raw	64.8	223	17.9	16.0
Beaver: cooked, roasted	56.2	248	29.2	13.7
Raccoon: cooked, roasted	54.8	255	29.2	14.5
Muskrat: cooked, roasted	67.3	153	27.2	4.1
Venison: Lean meat, raw	74.0	123	20.6	3.9
Rabbit: raw	59.8	218	29.5	10.1
Chicken: fryers, total edible, raw	53.3	189	23.3	13.0
Duck: wild, total edible, raw	61.1	233	21.1	15.8
Quail: total edible, raw	70.0	134	21.8	4.5
Frog legs:	81.9	73	16.4	0.3

Courtesy Alabama Cooperative Extension Service, Auburn University

Alabama's Wild Game

Dressing raccoon

Like the beaver, the 'coon has thick fat encasing his body to protect it from winter's frigid waters. This fat is strong in flavor and odor, so dress 'coons outdoors.

Begin the dressing process by flipping the 'coon over on its back and cutting off the feet (diagram No. 1, cuts No. 1 and No. 2). Make a cut through the skin, not the meat, at a rear leg (cut No. 3) and cut across to the other rear leg. Make a semi-circle cut (cut No. 4) around the anus connecting the cut on both ends to cut No. 3.

Drive a nail into a tree or barn and tie a rope around both rear legs and hang the animal (diagram No. 2) from the nail. Cut the bone in the tail and leave the tail connected to the pelt. Use a sharp knife to cut the skin away from the body and pull the skin downward as you go. After getting enough skin to get a good hold, use both hands and pull the skin all the way down to the front legs. Trim the skin from around the legs and pull the pelt down past the neck. After the hide is removed, you will notice, both by sight and smell, the thick fat. Saw off the head, being careful not to touch the fat.

Fill a 48-quart ice chest full of cold water and add 1 box of baking soda, 1 cup of vinegar and 1 cup of salt.

Soak the 'coon overnight and he'll come out the next morning smelling fresh. Scrape and cut off the fat and rewash the 'coon. Be especially careful to cut away kernels of fat under both legs. Cut 'coon into pieces and it's ready to cook.

NOTE: 'Coon parts are usually thick, so it's a good idea to parboil the pieces before cooking.

Alabama's Wild Game

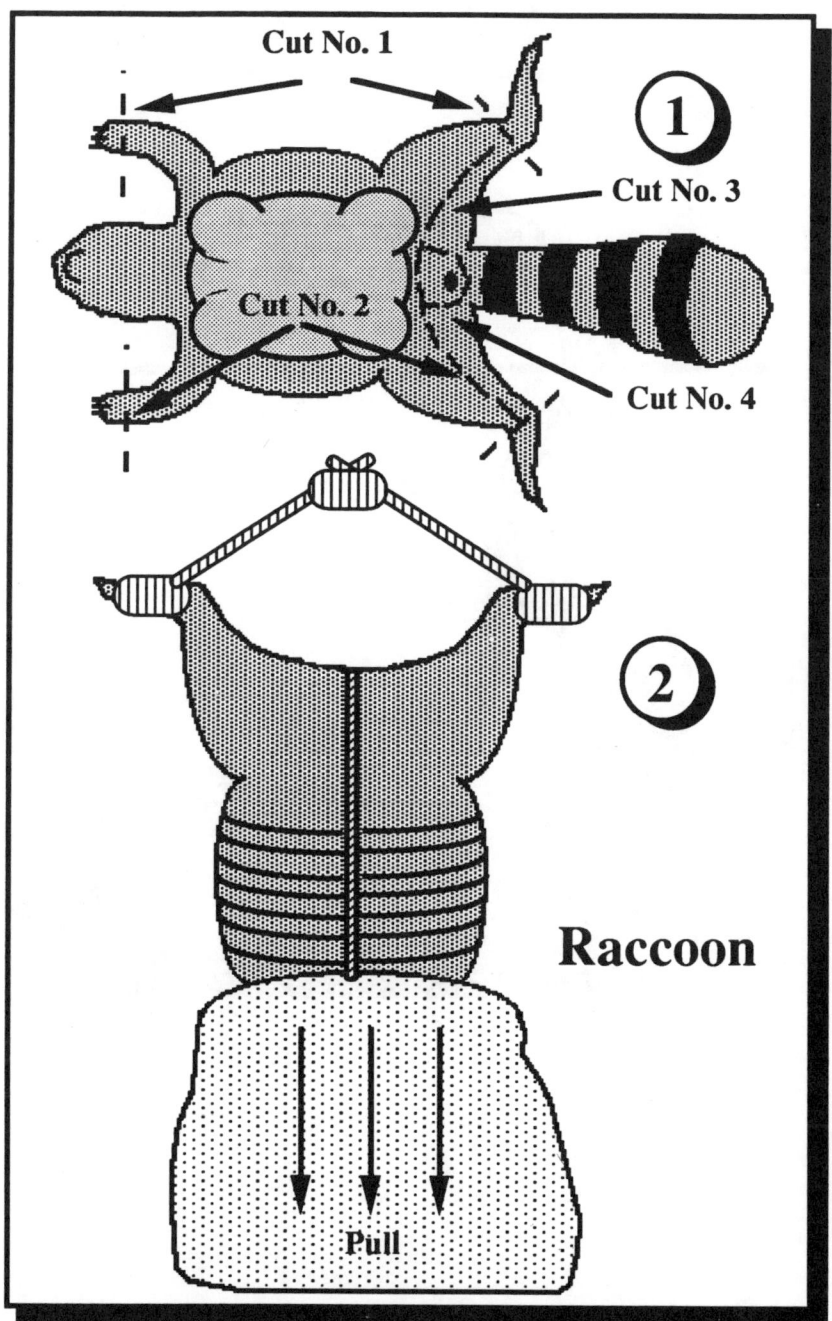

Raccoon

Alabama's Wild Game _____

Rattlesnake

The thought of being near a rattlesnake, much less eating one, sends chills up the spines of most people. That's a shame because the rattlesnake is one of Alabama's most valuable creatures, all the while being one of the less visible. Very few outdoorsmen can truthfully tell of a close call with a rattlesnake, although their embellished stories would hint otherwise.

Through all my years in the woods, I can honestly say I've never encountered one.

Rattlesnakes have the ability to tell the difference between a food they can handle, such as small rabbits and rodents, and human beings. They would rather slither away than deal with a human, and will bite only if provoked, or if they feel there is no escape. Their bites are almost never fatal and wasps and bees annually kill 10 times more people in the U.S. than snakes do. Most of those bitten by rattlesnakes are guilty of trying to handle them.

That said, let me admit I despise the thought of them. I'm careful to watch where I step in the woods, and if I ever did have a close encounter with one, I'd probably bypass the middle man and jump straight up to heaven. I'm the classic case of being a hypocrite.

One of my joys of living for three years in the south Alabama town of Elba was my annual early spring pilgrimage to nearby Opp for the Opp Jaycees Annual Rattlesnake Rodeo. It was there I first tasted fried rattlesnake and found what a delicacy it is. It is literally the finest-looking piece of meat you'll ever put in a skillet. It is whiter than chicken, and has a taste between chicken and a steak finger. The best way to describe it is that it tastes like rattlesnake.

All of the rattlesnakes found in Alabama are edible, but the larger ones are the easiest to clean and offer the most meat. Snakes shorter than two feet generally don't have enough meat to fool with.

I've cooked rattlesnake myself on several occasions with rattlesnakes given to me, or with rattlesnakes I've found hit by cars and still alive in the road. I've found it best not to tell anyone what they are eating until they have bragged on it.

Rattlesnake recipes

Opp-Fried Rattlesnake

1 pound of rattlesnake meat per person
1 quart of buttermilk
2 cups of flour
Vegetable oil
Salt and pepper to taste

Soak snake steaks in buttermilk for at least four hours. Remove and salt and pepper to taste. Batter in flour and deep fry in vegetable oil until golden brown.

Chad Elmore, Opp. President Opp Jaycees

Rattlesnake Chili

1 lb. rattlesnake filets
1 small onion, chopped
1 teaspoon salt
1 can tomato sauce
3 tablespoons chili powder
1 can chili beans
1/4 teaspoon garlic salt
1/4 cup tomato paste
2 cups of water
2 tablespoons flour

Alabama's Wild Game

Cut rattlesnake filets into dice-size pieces and brown in skillet, adding chopped onion when snake is turning brown. Cook until onions are clear, then drain off excess oil. Add all ingredients except beans and flour. Cover and simmer for 1 hour, stirring every 10 minutes. Mix flour with water and make a paste and add to chili slowly while stirring. Add beans. Add water to desired consistency. Simmer another 15-20 minutes, stirring every 10 minutes. Serves 6.

Courtesy of Opp Jaycees

Gamecock Rattlesnake

1 rattlesnake cut into 3-inch pieces
1 cup corn starch
1 cup flour
1/4 cup lemon juice
1 egg, beaten
1/2 cup milk
Salt and pepper to taste
Vegetable oil

Soak rattlesnake pieces in lemon juice for 1 hour. Drain rattlesnake pieces and dip into mixture of beaten egg and milk. Remove rattlesnake meat from egg and milk mixture and batter in flour and corn starch mixed in paper bag.
Deep-fat fry in iron skillet. Serve with turnip greens.

New Brockton Athletic Boosters

Alabama's Wild Game

Oven-Baked Rattlesnake

1 large rattlesnake, cut into 3-inch pieces
1 tablespoon margarine
1 tablespoon flour
Seasoning salt
1 cup milk
1/4 pound fresh mushrooms, sliced
1 teaspoon basil
1 teaspoon black pepper
1 tablespoon lemon juice

Place snake pieces in baking dish. Make sauce by melting butter and adding seasoning salt and flour. Slowly stir in milk until sauce is smooth. Pour sauce over meat and add mushrooms, basil, pepper and lemon juice. Cover and bake at 300 degrees for 1 hour.

Stir-Fry Rattlesnake

1 pound rattlesnake filets, cut into 1-inch strips
2 medium bell peppers, sliced into 1-inch strips
1 large onion, sliced
2 large carrots, cut into 1-inch strips
5 large mushrooms, sliced
1 can water chestnuts, drained
1 can bean sprouts, drained
1 cup of water
Vegetable oil
Dale's Steak Seasoning

Soak rattlesnake filets in mixture of 1/4 cup Dale's Steak Seasoning and 1 cup of water for 1 hour. Brown meat in vegetable oil in wok. Skillet will suffice if no wok is available. Remove meat and drain on paper towel. Heat oil to just before smoking stage. Add vegetables. Don't overcook. Remove vegetables while still crisp. Serve over white rice.

Pam Best, Birmingham

Alabama's Wild Game

Alabama's Wild Game

Dressing rattlesnake

The first step in dressing rattlesnake is the most obvious - remove the head (diagram 1, cut No. 1). Cutting the head off three inches behind the back of the head insures the venom sacks are removed and that they pose no danger. Dispose of the head where children and pets, especially dogs, can't find it. Then cut off the rattles (cut No. 2).

Flip the snake on its back (diagram 2). Slide the tip of an old pair of sharp scissors into the body opening where the head was. Cut the body cavity lengthwise (cut No. 3) from the neck area all the way to the anus. Extract the insides with your fingers.

Flip the snake back on its belly, and with a pair of pliers, grip the snake skin in the tail area and pull it off. It comes off easily.

The next step depends on how you intend to cook the snake. If you want to stir fry or make rattlesnake chile, filet the snake (diagram 3). Run a filet knife the length of the snake being careful to bounce the knife off the rib bones. Surprisingly, you lose very little meat this way.

If you plan to fry the snake like chicken, save yourself some time and effort and cut the snake into "snake steaks," or sections about three or four inches long (diagram 4). This requires a sharp knife because you must cut through the backbone.

Be sure to wash all snake meat in cold water and cut out and throw away any bloodshot or black meat. Chances are that is where the snake was bitten by another snake.

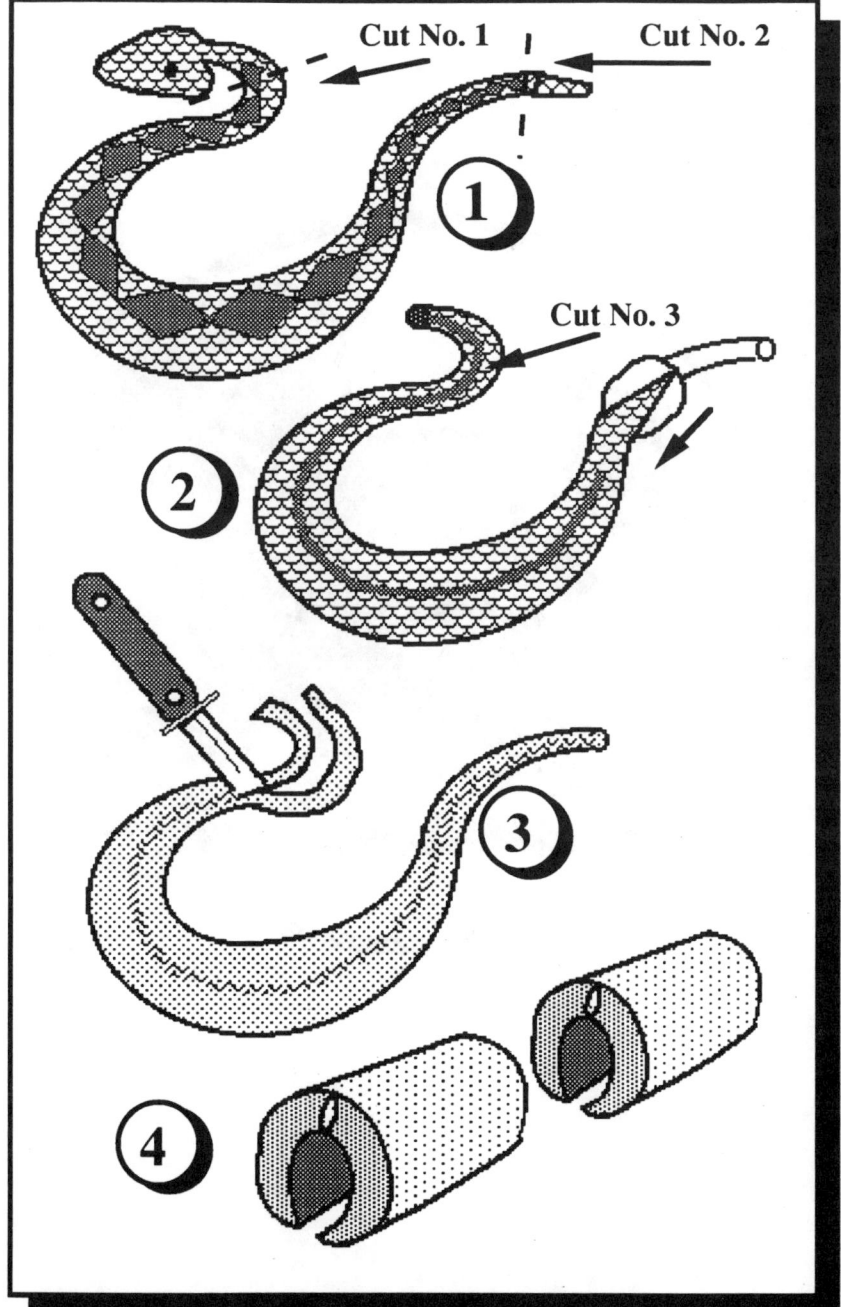

Alabama's Wild Game _____

Alabama's Wild Game

Squirrel

There's no question that the whitetail deer is the No. 1 hunted species of game animal in Alabama today. But less than 25 years ago, that title belonged to the gray squirrel.

The chattering little bushytail is the animal most Alabama hunters cut their teeth on. A poll of Alabama hunters would likely find their most memorable moments hunting came not while deer hunting, but on the crisp fall afternoons of their youth when they had a .22 rifle or a single shot shotgun and their dads or grandads at their side.

Squirrel hunting is still big time in Alabama and is one of the few survivors of the onslaught of deer hunting. While large parcels of land are needed for deer hunting, turkey hunting, rabbit hunting and quail hunting, a quarter-mile stretch of creek bank will often provide a limit of squirrels for the lucky hunter. Landowners who refuse to allow deer hunters on their property often have a soft spot in their hearts for squirrel hunters.

Squirrels, besides offering challenging hunting, are delicious eating. The meat is pink to medium red in color, and tender. Only the oldest squirrels, which there are not many of, require parboiling or pressure cooking to make them tender.

Alabama's Wild Game

Squirrel recipes

Basic Fried Squirrel

1 squirrel per person
1/2 cup milk
1 egg, beaten
Flour
Vegetable oil
Salt and pepper, to taste

Mix beaten egg and milk. Salt and pepper squirrel quarters and dip into mixture, then roll in flour. Place in hot oil and cook until golden brown, turning once.

Squirrel in Mushroom Gravy

4 squirrels, quartered
1/2 cup milk
1 egg, beaten
Salt and pepper, to taste
2 cans Campbell's Cream of Mushroom soup

Prepare squirrel just as you would for basic fried squirrel (above). Drain squirrel quarters on paper towel, then place in baking dish. In a separate bowl mix mushroom soup with 2 cans of water. Mix well. Pour over squirrel at 325 degrees for 2 hours.

Squirrel Stew

4 squirrels, quartered
2 cups tomato juice
1 can tomato paste
1 large onion, chopped
1 bag frozen mixed vegetables
Garlic salt, to taste
Hot sauce, to taste

Place frozen vegetables in a large pan, and cover with water and bring to boil. Add remaining ingredients, including squirrel.

Cover and simmer for three hours, adding tomato juice whenever necessary. Quartered potatoes may be added if not included in mixed vegetables.

Grilled Squirrel Supreme

4 squirrels, quartered
1/2 cup Dale's Steak Seasoning
1/4 cup cooking sherry
1/4 cup molasses or honey
1 tablespoon Liquid Smoke
Garlic salt, to taste
1 stick margarine

Place all ingredients in saucepan and stir over low heat until thoroughly mixed (about 5 minutes). Place squirrels in mixture and allow to sit for at least two hours. Move to grill and cook over hickory chips.

Alabama's Wild Game

Dressing squirrel

The hide of a squirrel is tougher to remove than most other game animals found in Alabama, but the old "one-minute-method" will allow you to dress a bunch of squirrels in no time flat.

Start by making a 2-inch cut through the skin under the tailbone (diagram No. 1). Place the squirrel on its stomach on the ground and step on the rear legs, grasp the tail, straighten up and pull the hide up the body and over the head and the front legs. Pick the squirrel up and pull the hide off of the rear of the body by pulling it over the hips and down the rear legs. Cut off the rear feet and the attached hide first, then the head and front feet. Place the squirrel on its back and make a cut from the anus to the neck (diagram No. 3) and remove the insides. Cut the squirrel into quarters (diagram No. 4) and wash thoroughly.

Alabama's Wild Game

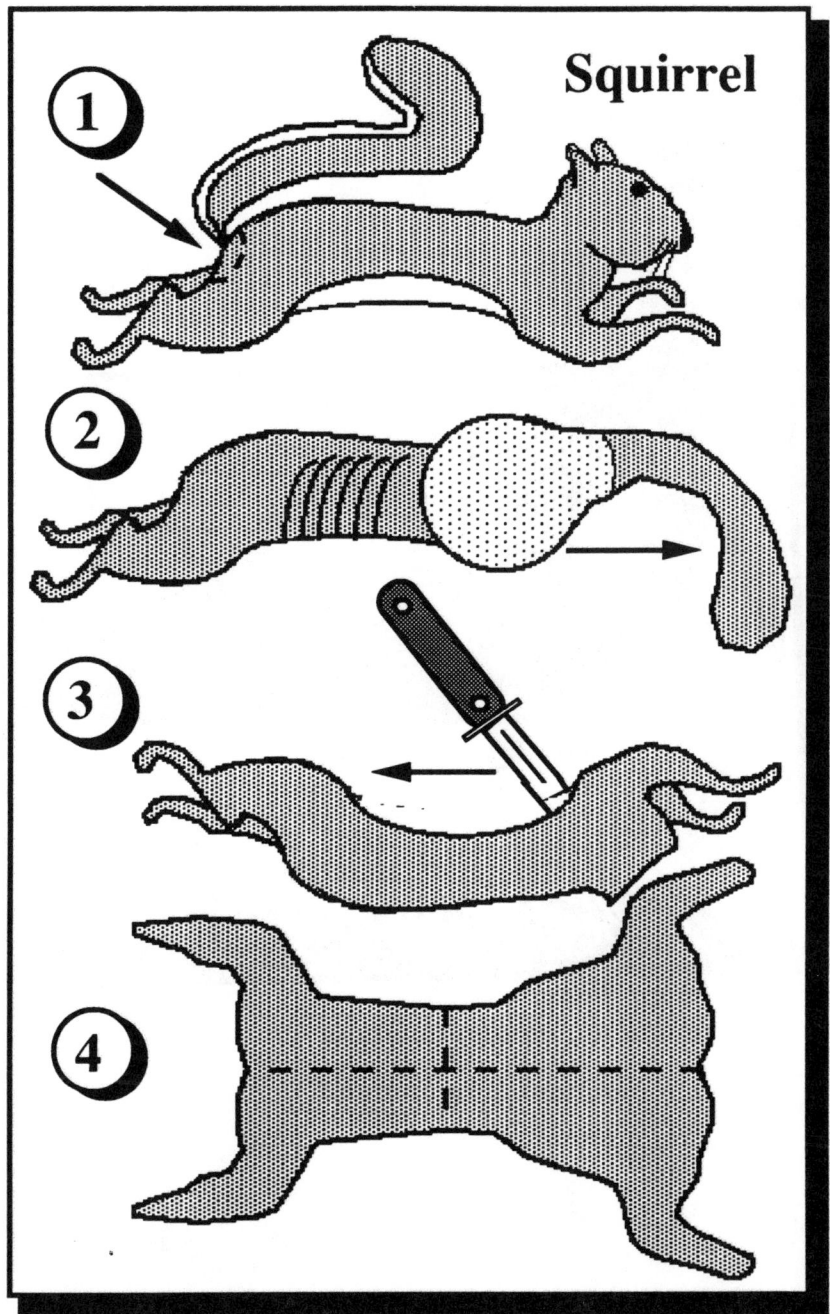

Alabama's Wild Game _____

Alabama's Wild Game

Wild Turkey

The re-establishment of large numbers of wild turkey in Alabama's forests is one of the truly great wildlife comeback stories of our time. The relatively recent resurgence of great numbers of the wily old bird has not only means a new challenge for a whole generation of new hunters, it also means the availability of a healthy and delicious wild game meat well worth the effort needed to outsmart old tom.

Unregulated hunting and overharvesting during the 1930's and 1940's nearly wiped out the wild turkey population not only in Alabama, but across the nation. The decline in wild turkey population in Alabama called for drastic measures including a major restocking program that put many restocked counties off limits to turkey hunting for five years.

Thankfully, those days are over. Alabama now has a wild turkey population estimated at a quarter-million strong and turkey hunting is now big business in the state.

Alabama's Wild Game

Wild Turkey Recipes

Eddie Salter's Fried Turkey Fingers

2 filets from one wild turkey breast
2 eggs, beaten
1 cup of milk
Flour
Salt and pepper, to taste
Vegetable oil

Cut breast meat into fingers and soak in mixture of milk and beaten eggs for 1 hour in refrigerator. Remove and salt and pepper to taste. Batter in flour. Heat vegetable oil until right before it smokes. Fry fingers quickly on both sides so they don't lose their moisture.

Eddie Salter, Brewton

Eddie Salter's Turkey Salad

This is where Eddie Salter's turkey legs, thighs and other dark meat end up.

Dark meat pieces of wild turkey
1 medium-size jar pimentos
1 tablespoon sugar
5 eggs, boiled, chopped
1 bell pepper, diced
1 stalk of celery, diced
1 small onion, diced
1 cup mayonnaise
2 salad pickles, diced
Salt and pepper, to taste

Boil turkey pieces until done. Scoop off top layer of broth and save. Allow turkey pieces to cool, then debone. Chop meat into pieces and add all ingredients except mayonnaise and broth. Add 1/2 cup broth and stir in desired amount of mayonnaise.

Eddie Salter, Brewton

Deep Fried Turkey

1 wild turkey breast
Vegetable oil to fill fish cooker

Heat oil in cooker until paper match laying in oil on the bottom of the cooker bursts into flames. Slowly lower breast into cooker and cook until outside is dark brown. Unbelievably simple - unbelievably good!

The late Ben Rogers Lee, Coffeeville

Simple Baked Turkey Breast

1 turkey breast
1 stick of margarine
2 apples, unpeeled
2 large onions, peeled
2 stalks celery, whole

Melt margarine and give turkey breast a good rubdown. Place on rack in roaster. Place apples, onions and celery on rack. Add 1 inch of water to roaster. Cover and place in oven preheated to 500 degrees. Cook 1 hour and turn oven off and leave overnight. Do not open door.

Mike and Beth Bolton, Argo

Smoked Turkey Breast on the Grill

1 turkey breast
2 cups white vinegar
2 cups red wine
Garlic salt, to taste
Seasoning salt, to taste
Hickory chips

Soak hickory chips in water at least 24 hours. Dip breast in cold water and sprinkle with garlic salt and seasoning salt. Place pan filled with vinegar and red wine under rack on one side of covered gas grill. Light opposite burner and place hickory chips on rack above fire. Place turkey breast on side with no fire, meat side up. Cook on low heat for 6 hours.

Mike and Beth Bolton

Alabama's Wild Game

Dressing Wild Turkey

Two-time world turkey calling champion Eddie Salter of Brewton is one of the world's best at dressing a turkey. Here's how he does it:

Method No. 1 - About 80 percent of the meat of a wild turkey is on the breast, so many hunters choose to avoid the hassle of plucking the bird by utilizing the breast only. If that's the case with you, place a rope around the turkey's neck (diagram No. 1) and hang him from a limb. Clip off the wings at the joint (cut No. 1), then, starting at the neck, insert a sharp knife between the skin and the breast (cut No. 2) and make a cut down to the anus. With short strokes of the knife, separate the skin from the breast to reveal the whole breast. Trim the breast meat away from the neck, breastbone and legs. This will give you two large pieces of meat. Wash thoroughly.

Method No. 2 - If you plan to use the whole turkey, as for baking, begin by boiling several pans of water. Place the whole turkey in a 5-gallon bucket and pour the boiling water over him (diagram No. 2). Add a couple teaspoons of dish washing detergent to the water. This helps to penetrate the oily feathers. Allow the turkey to sit a few minutes, then pluck him clean. Pat him dry with a towel and use a burning piece of rolled up newspaper to burn off the pin feathers. Cut off the head (diagram No. 3, cut No. 1), then cut a large hole around the anus (cut No. 2) and pull out the intestines. Reach in with your hand and pull out the remaining insides. Wash the whole bird thoroughly in cold running water, paying careful attention to the body cavity.

Alabama's Wild Game

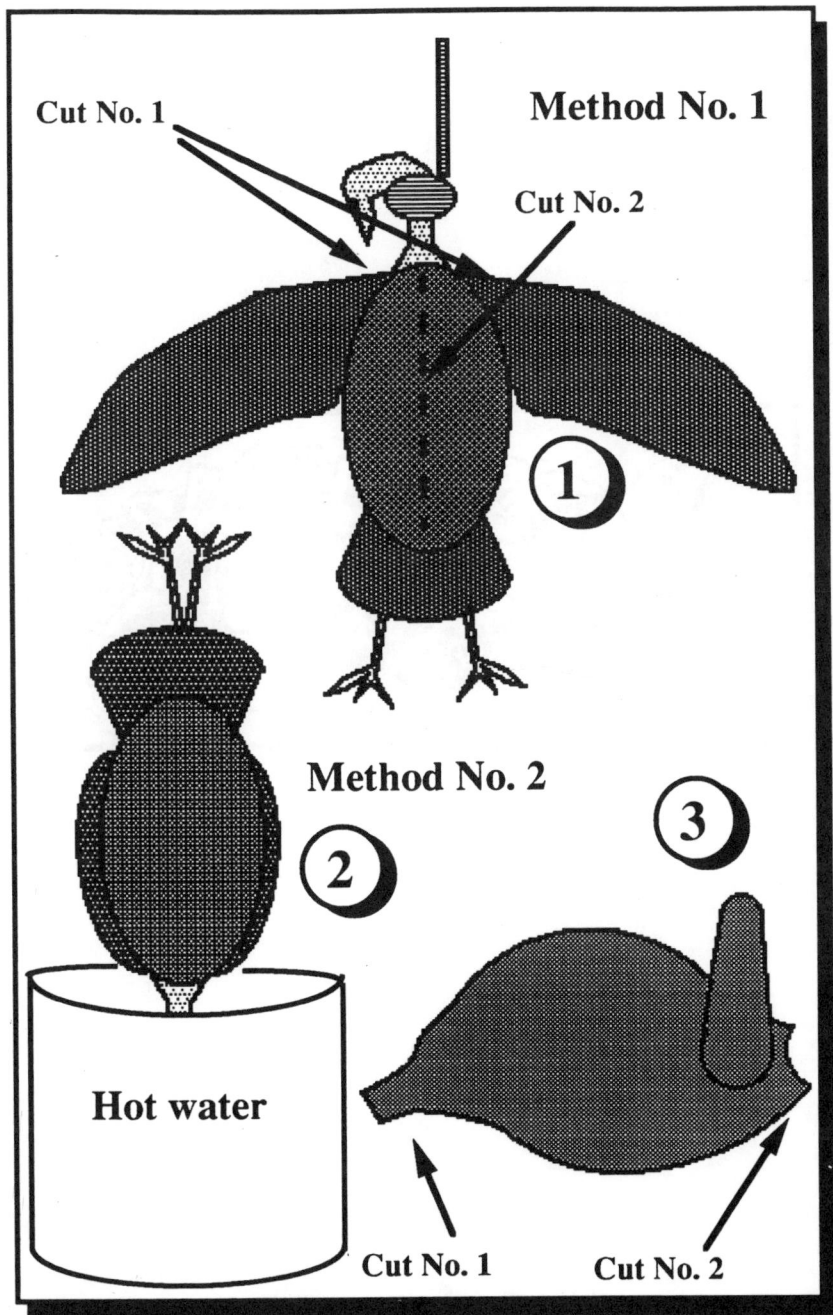

Alabama's Wild Game _____

Alabama's Wild Game

Turtle

Much is made of Alabama's estimated 1.3 million-strong deer herd and it is indeed impressive, but with 1/10 of the nation's fresh water flowing through Alabama, plus an estimated 30,000 private lakes in the state, our turtle herd ain't bad, either.

Turtles are everywhere in Alabama, but they are largely ignored as a food source. That's too bad, because everything the Good Lord made hard to get is good eating. Shrimp, lobsters and oysters are proof of that. Turtles are tough to clean, but once inside the shell, the wild game chef will find a variety of meat and it's all good eating.

Turtles may be the only wild animals in Alabama that landowners are glad to get rid of. Catching turtles is relatively easy, too. There are several ways to catch turtles, but one stands out above the rest - the turtle trap.

Start by making a square box (4-foot-square) from treated 2x4's. Cover three sides with some type of galvanized fencing small enough that the turtles can't escape. Place the box on the ground with the open side up and measure across the inside perimeter of the frame. Cut a 2x6 that length.

Drill a hole on each side of the top rail of the frame and drive a nail through the hole and into the end of the 2x6. Do the same on the other side. When finished, the 2x6 should stretch across the inside of the frame and should spin. Wire 4 1/2-gallon milk jugs to the corners of the upper frame and place a rock in the

Alabama's Wild Game

bottom (you'll need to experiment with rock size).

Place the trap in the lake or river and secure it in place. It should float with the top even with the water. When a turtle walks out on the 2x6 to sun itself, the 2x6 will roll and roll him off in the basket. He can't get out.

Turtle recipes

Basic Fried Turtle Strips

1 turtle per person
1/2 cup milk
1 egg, beaten
Flour
Vegetable oil
Salt and pepper, to taste

Mix beaten egg and milk. Salt and pepper turtle cubes, dip into mixture, then roll in flour. Place in hot oil and cook until golden brown, turning once.

Turtle Stew

2 pounds turtle meat, cubed
1 teaspoon garlic salt
2 cups tomato juice
3 large potatoes, diced
1/4 cup Dale's Steak Seasoning
1 can tomato paste
1 large onion, chopped
1 bag frozen mixed vegetables
Garlic sauce, to taste
Hot sauce, to taste

Place frozen vegetables in a large pan, and cover with water and bring to boil. Add remaining ingredients, including turtle meat. Cover and simmer for three hours, adding tomato juice whenever necessary.

Alabama's Wild Game

Dressing turtle

Start by nailing the turtle to a tree through the throat (diagram No. 1). Use a sharp hatchet to gently cut down the middle of the shell. Don't smash the shell, cut it. Once you cut through the length of the shell, use your fingers to pry open the shell (diagram No. 2). Use a filet knife to separate the body from the shell. Split the turtle open from the the neck to the anus and remove the insides. Cut off the head, feet and tail. Cut him into small pieces after washing.

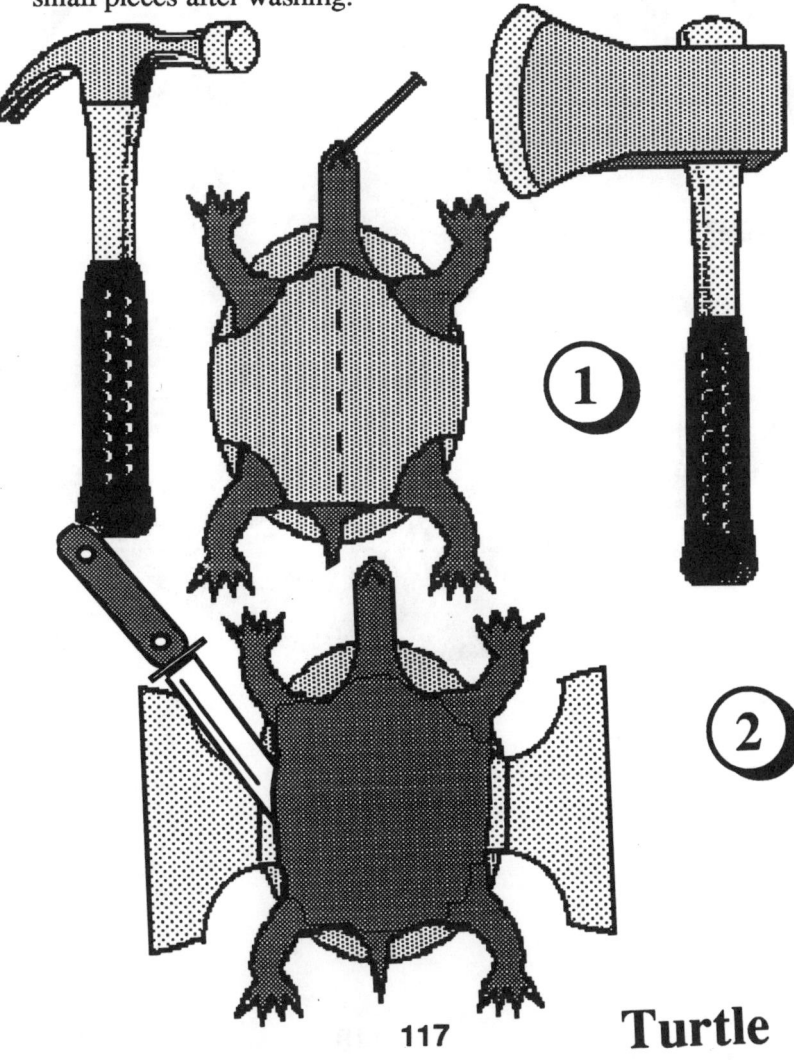

Turtle

Alabama's Wild Game _____

Venison

With a deer herd estimated at 1.3 million and a liberal bag limit which allows hunters to take a buck a day from mid-November to the end of January, it's no surprise that deer hunting in Alabama is big business - a multi-million dollar business.

A study by Auburn University has shown that 40 of Alabama's 67 counties receive major economic impact from deer hunting.

Alabama's deer herd is estimated at 1.3 million, which is more deer than the whole United States had in the 1920's. An estimated 200,000 deer hunters harvest 250,000 deer annually in Alabama.

That's a lot of venison, enough that deer processing plants thrive throughout Alabama.

Non-hunters often have problems understanding the joy of deer hunting, but fact of the matter is that a hunter who harvests two or three deer per season has filled his freezer with hundreds of pounds of quality meat which can feed his family throughout the year. A trophy for the wall is just gravy.

How many times have non-hunters gathered around my family's table and unknowingly eaten venison, proclaiming it one of the best meals they've ever eaten? How many times have the citizens of Argo eaten my chili at the annual Argo Volunteer Fire Department Chili Cook-Off and boasted of its wonderfulness, not knowing the main ingredient was venison?

Alabama's Wild Game

I find it strange when someone declares that venison has a "gamey" or "bloody" taste, for the venison I prepare does not have a hint of offensive, or even unusual, flavor. Of course, I know why some venison has such a flavor and mine doesn't - poor preparation.

Deer use their muscles more than cattle and as a result the meat is leaner and a bit more course, but that can be easily corrected by proper cooking. The "gamey" or "bloody" taste people talk about is a result of poor handling during the period between when the deer was shot and when it was removed from the freezer.

When any animal dies, its blood no longer circulates and it loses the ability to regulate the body temperature. This is especially critical in a large-bodied animal such as a deer where heat builds up in the muscle mass and major organs. A deer begins spoiling the second it dies.

Even if the weather is cold or cool, the heat transfers from the organs and muscles to the surrounding meat. In warm temperatures, this process is rapid.

Field dressing is a procedure that too many hunters ignore in this day and time. Hunters routinely are placed in their tree stands before daylight with an agreement to be picked up at 11 a.m. or noon. Most of these hunters carry no cleaning kit, or even a knife. Should that hunter kill a deer at 6 a.m., it may be 1 p.m. before the deer is removed from the woods and returned to the camphouse where the processing can begin.

If a beef processing outfit were to butcher its meat six or hours after it was killed, it would have the U.S.D.A. and *60 Minutes* knocking at its door.

Venison Recipes

Ol' Buckmaster's Backstrap Steaks

1 backstrap
Lemon pepper, to taste
Dale's Steak Seasoning
Salt, to taste
Bacon

Cut backstrap into 6-inch lengths. Use a filet knife to cut top 1/8 inch off backstrap all over. This guarantees removal of all fat and sinew. Pound backstrap hard with meat hammer or puncture it clear through with knife. Submerge in mixture of 1 part Dale's to 1 part water. Soak overnight. Remove, shake dry and sprinkle with lemon pepper and salt. Cut into steaks 1-inch thick and wrap bacon around each steak, securing with toothpicks. Grill over burned-down coals until inside is light pink. Cook rare or medium-rare only. Anything else will dry meat out too much.
Jackie Bushman, founder of "Buckmasters"

Davey Allison's Grilled Teriyaki Tenderloin

NASCAR's Davey Allison is an accomplished hunter who often cooks the wild game he harvests. Here's his favorite recipe:

1 venison tenderloin
1 8-ounce bottle Teriyaki sauce

Cut tenderloin into 6-inch lengths. Place in bowl and cover with Teriyaki sauce. Marinate overnight, turning pieces in mixture several times. Place coals in grill to one side, light and allow to burn down to glowing embers. Place tenderloin on grill's cool side and cover grill. Cook 20 minutes. Turn over, baste with Teriyaki sauce; cover again and cook 30 minutes.
Davey Allison, Hueytown

Alabama's Wild Game

Dale Earnhardt's Grilled Tenderloin

NASCAR's Dale Earnhardt and Davey Allison are competitive in everything they do, whether it's racing, hunting or recipe-giving. Earnhardt said to throw Davey's recipe away and use this one because it's easier and better:

1 venison tenderloin
1 bottle Italian dressing

Slice tenderloin into 1-inch-thick steaks. Fill bowl with bottle of dressing. Place tenderloin steaks into mixture and marinate overnight. Remove when it's time to cook and wrap bacon around edges of steaks and pin with toothpicks. Don't allow charcoal to burn down in grill because you need a hot fire. Add hickory chips soaked overnight in water. Place steaks on grill and cook quickly so venison won't dry out.

Dale and Theresa Earnhardt, Kannapolis, N.C.

Patti's Tenderloin

1 venison tenderloin
Dale's Steak Seasoning
1 pound bacon
Garlic salt, to taste
Salt and pepper, to taste

Cut tenderloin into steaks 3/4-inch thick. Tenderize by cross-cutting approximately half way through meat on each side (horizontal one way, vertical the other). Wrap each steak with one slice of bacon and pin with several toothpicks. Sprinkle steaks with garlic salt and salt and pepper. Marinate overnight in a mixture of 2 parts of Dale's Steak Seasoning to 1 part of water. Cook on hot grill approximately 4 minutes on each side, being careful not to overcook.

Patti Moultrie, Moultrie Feeders, Vestavia

Easy Grilled Tenderloin

1 venison tenderloin
2 large onions, sliced

Garlic salt, to taste
Bacon

Trim away all fat, but leave tenderloin whole. Soak tenderloin overnight in container of water in refrigerator to remove excess blood. Place tenderloin white sinew down on cutting board. Using a filet knife, cut into sections 6 inches long. Filet away sinew from each section. Allow coals in grill to burn down. Sprinkle garlic salt on each section (optional) and lay a slice of onion on each piece. Lay a strip of bacon lengthwise on section. Turn tenderloin frequently replacing onion and bacon each time. Cook for approximately 45 minutes. Cut into meat when it appears done. There should be a hint of pink approximately the size of a nickel in the center when the meat is perfect. Remove and slice into medallions 1/2-inch thick.

Doug Schofield, Opp, Ala.

Smack Your Mamma Tenderloin

Dan Moultrie, of Moultrie Feeders said this recipe will make you want to smack your Mamma because she didn't cook this for you all your life.

1 venison tenderloin
1/2 bottle Dale's Steak Seasoning
Garlic salt, to taste
Salt and pepper, to taste
Flour
1 Vidalia onion
Water
Vegetable oil

Cut tenderloins into steaks 3/4-inch thick. Tenderize by cross-cutting steaks half way through on both sides (horizontal one side, vertical the other). Season each steak with garlic salt and salt and pepper. Marinate overnight in mixture or 2 parts Dale's to 1 part water. Remove from marinade and set marinade aside. Flour each steak in hot oil and drain on paper towel. Add 1 cup of marinade mixture to drippings and stir. Add flour to thicken gravy. Return meat to gravy and cover with onion slices. Cover and simmer for 1 1/2 hours on low heat.

Dan Moultrie, Moultrie Feeders, Vestavia

Alabama's Wild Game

Grilled Turkey Bacon Deer Meat

1 pound venison, cut into 1-inch cubes
1 cup Dale's Steak Seasoning
1 cup red wine
1/4 cup lemon juice
1 pound turkey bacon

Wash deer meat in cold water, then soak in cold water for two hours. Mix lemon juice, steak sauce and wine for marinade. Soak deer meat in this mixture for at least three hours. Remove meat and wrap each piece with turkey bacon. Place on grill over medium heat. Meat is done when bacon is done.

Maybelle Gunter, Jasper

Smoked Venison Tenderloin

2 whole tenderloins
4 strips bacon
3 cups red wine
Black pepper, to taste

Remove all fat and sinew from tenderloins. Sprinkle with black pepper and place two strips of bacon on each tenderloin. Prepare smoker as usual and add wine to water bowl (this gives eat a nice color around edges when sliced.) Smoke 3 to 4 hours on medium heat. Be careful not to overcook.

Ben D. King, Columbiana

Marinated Deer Steaks

2 pounds deer tenderloin
1 large bottle Zesty Italian salad dressing
1 package Lipton's Onion Soup mix

Slice tenderloin into 1-inch steaks. Mix Italian dressing and soup in large bowl. Place steaks in bowl and coat well. Cover and marinate for at least three hours. Place on grill and cook medium well. Don't overcook.

Paula Calloway, Pat's Archery, Jasper

Moultrie's Killer Camphouse Venison Roast

1 hindquarter
1 package Lipton's Onion Soup
1/2 bottle worcestershire sauce
2 beef bouillon cubes dissolved in 1 cup of water
Lemon pepper, to taste
Salt and pepper to taste

Cut shank from hindquarter. Place roast under cold running water and shake dry. Sprinkle with salt and pepper and lemon pepper. Place in roaster. Pour all ingredients over roast with soup mixture going on last. Cover and cook at 300 degrees for 4 hours. Marinate roast every 30 minutes while cooking.

Dan Moultrie, Moultrie Feeders, Vestavia

Venison Neck Roast

This is a good reason to save the neck portion that is usually thrown away.

1 venison neck roast
1 package Lipton's Onion Soup
Garlic powder
Salt and pepper, to taste
1 teaspoon dried parsley flakes
1 teaspoon oregano
1/2 teaspoon sweet basil

Place large sheet of aluminum foil in bottom of pan. Add 1-inch of water. Wash neck roast and sprinkle with remaining ingredients. Wrap tightly in foil and bake at 350 degrees for 2 hours.

Sunday Dinner Venison Roast

1 hindquarter
Garlic cloves, to taste
Celery seed, to taste
Black pepper, to taste
2 medium onions, sliced
2 cups Dale's Steak Seasoning
1/2 cup instant coffee
1/2 lb. bacon
Salt and pepper, to taste
Small onions
Carrots
Small potatoes
1 cup vegetable oil
1/2 cup white vinegar

Remove all sinew and fat. Make splits in top of roast large enough for split garlic cloves to be slid into. Place roast in roaster. Pour 1 cup of vegetable oil over top of roast followed by 1/2 cup vinegar. Salt and pepper to taste, and sprinkle with celery seed. Place onion slices over top of roast and drape bacon slices over the top of onions. Add water to pan to a depth of 1 inch. Add 2 cups of Dale's Steak Seasoning and 1/2 cup instant coffee. Cover roaster and cook at 300 degrees for 4 1/2 hours. Baste each hour with drippings. At approximately 45 minutes before being done, add onions, potatoes and carrots.

Mike and Beth Bolton, Argo

Venison Breakfast Steaks

Steaks cut from deboned hindquarter or tenderloin
1 tablespoon dried mustard
1 tablespoon cornstarch
1/2 cup flour
Salt and pepper, to taste
Vegetable oil

Mix mustard, four and cornstarch in paper bag and shake well. Wet steaks and batter in mixture. Take meat hammer and pound ingredients into meat to tenderize. Cook quickly in hot oil.

Venison in Sherry Sauce

Venison steaks cut from hindquarter or backstraps
2 cups cooking sherry
1 large onion, cut into 1/2-inch rings
3 cups sour cream

Simmer cooking sherry in electric skillet. Add onions and sour cream. Mix well. Add steaks and cover. Simmer for 1 hour.

Noel Feather

Crock Pot Venison Barbecue

1 small venison roast
1 large onion, quartered
2 packages Lipton Onion Soup mix
4 strips bacon
Pinch of fennel
Pinch of dill
Salt and pepper, to taste
Garlic salt, to taste
Barbecue sauce of choice
Brown sugar

Wrap roast in bacon strips and secure with toothpicks. Place in crock pot. Add onion soup mix, fennel, dill, salt and pepper, garlic salt and onion. Fill crock pot half full of water, cover, and cook on medium heat until the meat will pull off the bones easily. Allow to cool until you can handle meat. Remove meat from bones and place in baking dish. Cover with barbecue sauce and sprinkle on brown sugar.

Woody Ward, Union City, Ga.

Alabama's Wild Game

Barbecued Venison Chops

2 pounds venison chops
1 medium onion, chopped
1/2 cup celery, chopped
2 tablespoons margarine

Brown chops in margarine in skillet. Saute onions and celery. Place chops and sauteed onions and celery in baking dish and cover with favorite barbecue sauce. Cook at 350 degrees for about 1 1/2 hours.

Venison Fajitas

This recipe will keep you from throwing away the rib meat on future deer.

3 pounds rib meat
Garlic salt, to taste
Salt and pepper, to taste
1/4 cup Dale's Steak Seasoning
2 tablespoons vegetable oil

While deer is being processed, place a filet knife between two rib bones and cut away strip of meat between the ribs. Cut away all the meat this way. Label it "Fajitas" on the wrapping paper and freeze in 3-pound packs. Thaw 1 pack and sprinkle strips with salt, pepper and garlic salt. Heat vegetable oil in skillet and add Dale's. Cook strips until tender. Use as fajita meat.
Mike and Beth Bolton, Argo

Stir Fry Venison No. 1

1 pound venison, cubed
2 bell peppers, sliced
2 stalks celery, chopped
1/2 pound mushrooms, sliced
4 carrots, cut into 4-inch sticks
2 tablespoons bacon drippings
2 medium onions, chopped
Garlic salt, to taste
1 stalk broccoli, chopped

Alabama's Wild Game

3 tablespoons Dale's Steak Seasoning
1/4 cup red wine
1 stick margarine

Debone venison cut off your choice. Trim away fat and sinew. Soak meat in clear water in refrigerator overnight to remove excess blood. Cut into bite-size cubes. Melt margarine in wok or skillet and add garlic salt, wine and bacon drippings. Heat to a stable temperature and add meat and vegetables. Stir continuously to give each piece its turn at the heat. Don't overcook. Keep meat tender and vegetables crisp.

Doug Schofield, Opp Ala.

Stir Fry Venison No. 2

2 pounds venison, large ground chunks
2 large bell peppers, cut into strips
1 large onion, chopped
Salt and pepper, to taste
Garlic powder, to taste
1/2 cup soy sauce
1 egg, beaten
2 cups flour
Vegetable oil

Heat electric frying pan to 350 degrees. Saute onions and bell pepper until onions turn clear. In a large bowl, mix flour, meat, garlic powder, salt and pepper and egg. Mix well. Remove onions and bell pepper and add enough oil to cover bottom of skillet. Add meat and cover. Stir occasionally until done. Reduce heat to 250 degrees. Add onions and peppers, 1/4 cup of soy sauce, and season with salt and pepper and garlic salt. Cook 30 minutes, adding remaining soy sauce halfway through.

Christy Savage, Anniston

Tater Tot Venison Casserole

1 pound ground venison
1/2 onion, chopped
1 tablespoon vegetable oil
1/2 teaspoon salt
Salt and pepper, to taste
4 large potatoes, sliced
1 can Campbell's Cream of Mushroom soup

Brown ground venison in oil. Add salt and pepper. Slice potatoes and boil until tender. Drain. In a lightly greased baking dish, arrange layers of sliced potatoes, ground venison and soup. Top with frozen Tater Tots. Bake at 400 degrees for 35 minutes.

Ground Venison Loaf No. 1

1 pound ground venison - no fat
1 package saltine crackers, crushed
1 large onion, chopped
1 large tomato, chopped
4 tablespoons Dijon mustard
3 tablespoons jalapeno, crushed
2 tablespoons ground sage
2 eggs, beaten
1/3 cup Italian dressing
3/4 cup milk
1/2 teaspoon salt
1/2 teaspoon pepper

Mix all ingredients by hand in large bowl. Bake in loaf pan with foil on top for about 30 minutes at 350 degrees. Take foil off and bake 30 minutes until top is nicely browned and loaf is firm. Remove from oven and allow to cool for 15 minutes.

Susan Beck, Birmingham

Ground Venison Loaf No. 2

1 1/2 pounds ground venison
3/4 cup oatmeal, uncooked
1 cup evaporated milk

3 tablespoons onions, chopped
1 1/2 teaspoons salt
1/4 teaspoon pepper
3 tablespoons Dale's Steak Seasoning
3 tablespoons vinegar
2 tablespoons sugar
1 cup catsup

Mix all ingredients in large mixing bowl. Form into loaf. Place in loaf pan sprayed with Pam. Bake at 350 degrees until outside turns dark brown.

Venison Stroganoff

1 pound deboned front shoulder
1/4 cup margarine
1/2 pound fresh mushrooms
1 can beef broth
2 cups egg noodles
3/4 onion, chopped
Garlic salt, to taste
1 cup sour cream
2 1/2 tablespoons flour
Salt and pepper, to taste

Cut venison into 1-inch slices 1/8 inch thick; brown in butter, onions and garlic salt. Add mushrooms and saute. Heat beef broth to boil and add sour cream and flour. Simmer and stir until thickened. Mix everything, except noodles, in pan and simmer for two hours. Serve on cooked noodles.

Alabama's Wild Game

Venison Spaghetti Casserole

1 pound ground venison
12 ounces cooked spaghetti noodles
1 cup of whole milk
32-ounce jar of Ragu Chunky Spaghetti Sauce
2 cups Mozzarella cheese, grated
1 medium, chopped
1/4 cup margarine
2 eggs, beaten

Brown venison and onion in margarine. Mix eggs and milk. In a greased baking dish, make layers of spaghetti, eggs and milk mixture, spaghetti sauce and Mozzarella cheese. Bake for 45 minutes in 350 degree oven.

Venison Lasagna

1 pound ground venison
8 oz. lasagna noodles, cooked
1 medium onion, chopped
1 1/2 cups tomato juice
1/2 cup of water
1 teaspoon brown sugar
1/4 teaspoon garlic powder
1/2 teaspoon chili powder
1 small can tomato paste
8 ounces Mozzarella cheese
1 egg, beaten
8-ounce package cream cheese

Brown venison and onion; add salt and pepper to taste. Add all other ingredients except noodles, beaten egg and cream cheese. Lay noodles in greased baking dish. Add layer of ground venison. Add layer of cream cheese. Keep adding layers until everything's gone. Top with shredded cheese and cook in 350-degree oven for 40 minutes.

Field dressing

Being ready to field dress an animal takes no complex preparation. Fold a couple of garbage bags neatly around a sharp knife and a can of white pepper and secure it with rubber bands and place it in a jacket pocket and you're ready to go.

A good rule of thumb is that if it will be more than one hour before the animal can be moved to somewhere to be dressed, field dressing is needed.

Follow these directions:

1. A great trick I learned years ago was to start by sprinkling white pepper on the animal's nose, eyes, ears and mouth, then give a light coating of white pepper on its whole body. Flies, yellowjackets and other insects find white pepper offensive and keep their distance, which is most helpful. Swatting bugs with a sharp knife in hand can lead to field dressing yourself.

2. If possible, place the deer's legs uphill. This will keep the organs, intestines and stomach inside the deer where you want them while you make the preliminary cuts.

3. Make the first cut around the rectal cavity at the anal opening, freeing it from the surrounding tissues. Be especially careful not to cut the rectal tube.

4. On a buck, carefully cut around the penis and testicles, separating it from the surrounding tissues, being careful not to sever the tubes leading to the bladder.

5. Place a sharp knife, facing up, in the incision formed by the removal of the penis and make a cut all the way to the breastbone. This cut should be between the hide and skin and should not be made into the body cavity. Keeping the knife pointing up prevents it from dulling and also pulls hair away from the cut instead of forcing hair into the cut.

6. Pull the hide on both sides of the cut up and out of the way and make a cut, starting at the rectum, through the thin skin that holds in the intestines. Make the cut all the way to the breastbone, once again pointing the knife upward as not to cut into the stomach or intestines.

7. Reach into the cavity and cut away the diaphragm muscle which holds the insides in place, then reach into the neck and cut the jugular vein and airway.

8. Lay a plastic garbage bag onto the ground on the side opposite the legs and roll the deer over allowing the intestines

Alabama's Wild Game

and organs to roll out on the bag. Place all of the intestines and organs into the bag to be disposed of later. If keeping the liver, which you should, cut it away and lay it on another bag you have spread before you. It needs to cool quickly!

9. You may now cut through the diaphragm and remove the heart and lungs. If keeping the heart, which also is good eating, filet the heart into quarters, pour out the blood and cut out the valves. Place it beside the liver to cool.

10. Roll the deer on its stomach and pick it up, if possible, by the antlers or ears and by the tail to allow all blood to pour out. Make sure no dirt or debris enters the cavity. If it does, wipe it away. Break or cut a stick to prop open the body cavity to enhance cooling. If the weather is warm, drag the deer to the shade, if possible.

11. If you're taking the deer on more than an hour ride to be be butchered and the weather is above 40 degrees, placing several bags of ice into the cavity to keep it cool.

12. Never strap a deer on the hood of a vehicle because the engine heat will speed up the spoiling process. It will also notify the world you're the most uncaring redneck who has ever lived.

Aging venison

Many hunters believe in aging their meat, which isn't a bad idea if possible. Hanging a deer in a cooler with a constant temperature of 33 to 40 degrees for a week gives the meat better texture and flavor. The deer, with skin on, should be hanged by its rear legs and washed thoroughly to remove all blood and debris before placed in the cooler.

Skinning

Removing the hide of a deer is a necessity before it can be butchered. Keep in mind that one of the primary reasons for "gamey" tasting venison is the presence of hair, which gives venison a most unpleasant taste. Wash the deer thoroughly after removing the hide.

1. Make an incision in the thin skin between the tendon and the knee joint on each rear leg and place a gimbrel made for deer skinning between the legs. This spreads open the rear legs and

allows the deer to be elevated for better access.

2. With a sharp knife, once again pointed outwards, make a cut through the hide up the inside of each rear leg from the body cavity to the knee joint. Point the knife inward this time and as you pull the hide away from the skin, cut through the membranes which hold the hide to the skin. Trim away the hide up to the knee joints and all the way around to the tail.

3. Pull the tail downward and cut through the joint. Continue trimming the hide away. It's often possible at this point to pull the hide all the way down the back with a strong tug.

4. If the deer is to be mounted, cut a circle around the body behind the front legs and pull the cape down over the front legs as far as possible, saving as much cape as possible. Pull the hide down over the neck as far as possible, then cut off the head with a meat saw.

5. If the deer is not to be mounted, continue trimming the hide away off the front legs (to the knee joint) and pull the hide down to the head as far as possible. Cut off the head with a meat saw.

6. Cut off the front legs at the knee joint with a meat saw.

7. The deer is skinned at this point. Wash it thoroughly in cold water.

Butchering

How you butcher a deer depends a lot on how you plan to use the meat and which parts of the deer you plan to use.

Here's my way:

1. Pull the front shoulder downward. Using a sharp knife, start in the armpit and cut the meat down to the joint. Cut the meat all the way around the shoulder and pop the shoulder out of the socket. Repeat on the other front shoulder.

2. Cut the neck off at the base of the neck. Cut it lengthwise and remove the windpipe. The neck makes a good roast or stew meat.

3. Use a filet knife to cut out the backstraps, the long strips of meat along the spine. This is prime meat.

4. Use the filet knife to cut out the tenderloins, the strips of meat inside the cavity along the spine. This meat is no good. Wash it and freeze it and bring it to me so I can dispose of it for you. Just kidding. This is the best meat on the deer.

5. Use the filet knife to cut away the meat between each rib.

Many people throw this away, but it's great for fajitas or chili!

6. Cut through the spine just below the hips. Dispose of the hanging lower half.

7. Use the meat saw to cut down through the middle of the spine. This separates the two hams, or rear hindquarters. Remove the hams from the gimbrel and cut off the legs below the knee joints.

8. Wash each piece of meat thoroughly.

Deboning

Backstraps and tenderloins may be left whole or cut into pieces, but the hams and shoulders are often too large to put into a freezer. Deboning will save a lot of freezer space.

I always chose to debone, except for an occasional whole hindquarter which I smoke or use in a roast. Even then, I'm often forced to cut off the shank so it will fit on the grill or in the roaster.

How to prepare from here is matter of personal preference, but if the deer is exceptionally large or old, chances are it will be tough. Don't waste your time cutting steaks or roasts. Chop it fine for use in barbecue, grind it into hamburger or sausage, or cut it up for stew meat.

Here's a few pointers:

1. For gosh sakes, trim away as much fat as possible. Unlike beef fat which is flavorful, venison fat is bitter and leaves an awful aftertaste. Trim away all fat and sinew.

2. The most tender meat on a deer is the backstraps and tenderloins. The meat high on the rear legs is a close second. Use this meat for steaks.

3. The shanks, front shoulders and neck muscles are always tougher meat. Grind it into burgers or sausage, cut it up into stew meat or chop it fine for barbecue.

4. Wash the meat thoroughly before wrapping in a double layer of freezer paper and sealing with freezer paper. Label each package with what's in it and the date. Deer meat usually stays good for six to eights months in the freezer.

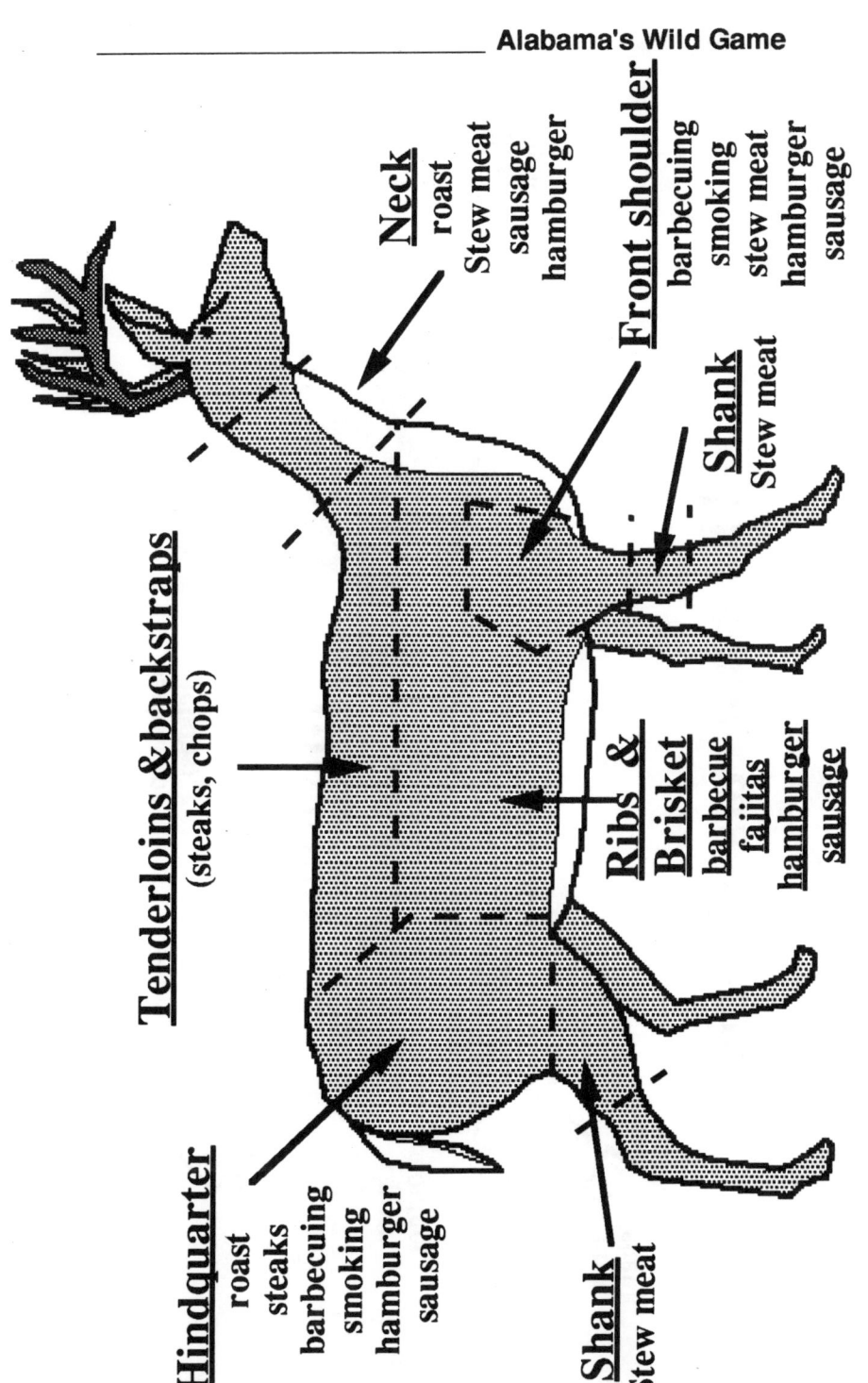

Alabama's Wild Game _____

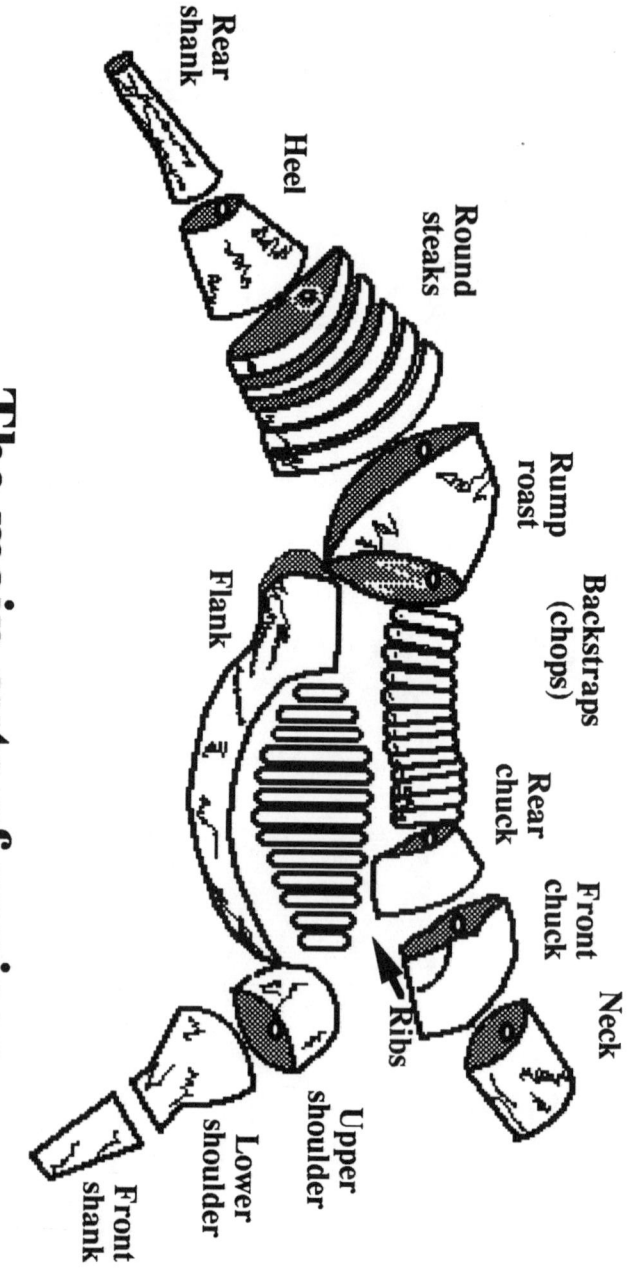

The main cuts of venison

Live deer weights

Hunters are often interested in knowing the live weight of the deer they harvest. The following table can give you an accurate figure based on the deer's weight after field dressing:

Field-dressed weight	Live or whole weight
50 pounds	63.5 pounds
60 pounds	76.2 pounds
70 pounds	89.0 pounds
80 pounds	101.7 pounds
90 pounds	114.4 pounds
100 pounds	127.2 pounds
110 pounds	139.9 pounds
120 pounds	152.6 pounds
130 pounds	165.3 pounds
140 pounds	178.0 pounds
150 pounds	190.7 pounds
160 pounds	203.4 pounds
170 pounds	216.1 pounds
180 pounds	228.8 pounds
190 pounds	241.5 pounds
200 pounds	254.2 pounds
210 pounds	266.0 pounds
220 pounds	279.6 pounds

Venison Jerky

Venison jerky is probably the only food I would be willing to eat every meal. I probably have eaten a ton of the stuff sitting in tree stands through the years.

Jerky-making is an age-old tradition begun by Indians so unrefrigerated meat could be kept for long periods of time. Today, jerky is more a snack food than a sustenance food. Most store-bought jerky is overly dry to enhance its shelf life, and it's filled with preservatives like monosodium glutamate and sodium nitrate for the same reason. Most store-bought jerky isn't that good. The venison jerky you can make has the potential to be rich in flavor, as well as chewable.

Anyone who eats store-bought jerky also knows that it's ridiculously over-priced. That's another of the benefits of making your own. Based on comparative stores prices, a full-sized deer will easily make $700 or $800 worth of jerky.

You'll be either smoking and drying venison jerky, so it will be preserved to some extent, but keep in mind that you won't be adding preservatives. Home made venison jerky should be kept frozen, in the refrigerator or on ice to keep it fresh as possible. It won't hurt to put it in your pocket before daylight and eat it in your tree stand at noon, but don't throw it in the back of the hot car on Friday afternoon and eat it on the way home Sunday afternoon.

Venison jerky recipes

Mike Bolton's Backstrap Jerky

1 backstrap
1 bottle Dale's Steak Seasoning
1 cup brown sugar
1 teaspoon paprika
Garlic salt, to taste
Onion salt, to taste
Coarse black pepper, to taste

Cut backstraps with the grain in strips 6 inches long, 1 inch wide and 1/2 inch thick. Mix 1 bottle of Dale's, 1 cup of brown sugar,

1 teaspoon paprika and sprinkle with garlic salt and onion salt to taste. Mix well. Marinate strips in this mixture all day. Remove strips and save marinade. Sprinkle strips with coarse black pepper to taste. Pour marinade into pan in smoker. Allow coals to burn down and drape strips over racks in smoker. Smoke 8 hours.

Mike Bolton, Argo

Rocco and Aleria's Oven Dried Jerky

1 venison hindquarter
3 cups Dale's Steak Seasoning
2 tablespoons black pepper

Cut venison into strips of desired length and width. Marinate all day in Dale's and Liquid Smoke. Remove from marinade. Pepper to taste. Place rack in oven at highest level and remove all other racks. Place aluminum foil in bottom of oven and curl edges to catch drippings. Run a toothpick through venison strips 1/4 inch from end and hang from rack allowing toothpicks to catch on rack. Put oven on lowest setting and block open oven door 1-inch. Dry jerky overnight.

Rocco and Aleria Lorino, Birmingham

Alabama's Wild Game

Making venison sausage

Venison sausage - whether it be a patty on the breakfast plate or stuffed sausage on the smoker or grill - is one of the great rewards of harvesting a deer. A deer hunter who doesn't take the time to learn the fun art of sausage-making is missing the boat.

Making your own sausage from venison has several benefits.

First, venison sausage is healthier than pork sausage because you control the fat content and it has no preservatives.

Because venison is so lean, you must mix some pork fat with it or it would fall apart when you grind it. Even if you could make it hold together, it wouldn't have enough fat to make a sizzle in the skillet. It would just dry up. But you still can produce a sausage that contains far less fat than the sausage you purchase from the local grocer.

Second, everyone has a particular taste they enjoy in sausage. Many like their sausage spicy and hot; others like their's plain or mild. By making your own, you control the flavor.

Purchasing a grinder

One of the best purchases you can make as a deer hunter is a meat grinder. It is useful not only in making sausage, but also for making hamburger meat. Grinders are available from butcher supply houses, or your local hardware store can likely order one for you.

They come in two types. Hand-operated and commercial. Hand-operated grinders and are usually $30 or less. Commercial grinders, which are electrically operated, usually start at $250 or more. The only reason you would ever need a commercial grinder is if your hunting club was sausage crazy.

Grinders usually come with three plates - course, medium and fine.

If you plan to make stuffed sausage, try to find one that has a sausage-stuffing attachment. That will save you some work later on.

Alabama's Wild Game

Patty or stuffed?

The first thing you must decide when making sausage is whether you want to make patties or stuffed sausage. Patties are the easiest because they don't require any special materials or effort. Many prefer stuffed sausage, however. Stuffed sausage is a must if you want sausage for the smoker or grill.

To make patties, simply use a rolling pin to roll out the product (after its mixed and seasoned, covered later in this chapter) on a piece of waxed paper. It's best to allow this to cool in the refrigerator for 30 minutes before using a cookie cutter to cut out the patties or it gets messy. Place about eight patties on another piece of wax paper, then put another piece of wax paper on top and add more patties. You can make as many layers as you want before freezing. After freezing the patties solid, they may then be wrapped in freezer paper or placed in sealable bags without fear they will stick together.

Making stuffed sausage is a bit more complicated.

You must locate the casings, which, in this day and time, is sometimes difficult. The butcher at your local grocery store can probably point you in the right direction. These casings usually come in large quantities and for this reason, you should plan to make a minimum of 30 pounds of stuffed sausage each time.

These casings come frozen and heavily salted. You must thaw them in cold water, then wash them thoroughly by running water through them before using them.

Chances are your grinder didn't come with a sausage-stuffing attachment, so you must make one. A neat trick I learned from Jeff Hadaway, a guide at Rockfence Station in Chambers County, is to unscrew the front ring of the grinder and drop it over the pointed end of an expensive aluminum funnel purchased at the grocery store or auto parts house. Use a felt-tip marker to draw a line around the bottom of the ring, then use tin shears to cut around the line. Place the ring back over the re-sized funnel and screw it back on the grinder. You now have a stuffing attachment.

To stuff sausage (after its thoroughly mixed and seasoned, covered later in this chapter) remove the strainer and add the funnel attachment. Grease the nipple with a piece of sausage so the delicate casing will slide on easily. Cut a casing to the length you desire (some may come six feet long) and slide one end onto the nipple. Slowly push the whole casing over the nipple. Pull about six inches of casing off the nipple and tie a knot in the end.

You may then begin putting cooled, nearly frozen mixed and seasoned sausage back into the grinder. It will automatically stuff the casing and pull it off the nipple as you crank.

You may want to stuff a 5-foot length of sausage for convenience, then cut it into 2 1/2-foot lengths so it's more manageable in the freezer.

Selecting the meat

Many people make sausage from what's left over from processing the deer and it's no doubt admirable to utilize the whole deer, but sausage is a delicacy. Using choice cuts from the shoulders and hams will result in a better product.

Begin by deboning the cuts, being careful to cut away all the fat, sinew and gristle. Cut into pieces small enough to go into your grinder.

As said before, venison is so lean it must be mixed with some fat to make sausage. What to mix the venison with is a matter of debate. Many venison sausage makers use beef fat, while others choose pork fat. Many have begun mixing it with the inexpensive bacon ends you find boxed at the grocery store. Bacon ends make a quality sausage.

Jeff Hadaway is unquestionably one of the finest sausage makers in the South. His choice is lean Boston butts or pork shoulders. That is a more expensive route, but take it from someone who has spent many hours at the Rockfence breakfast table. The result is worth the money. Jeff's theory is that you get moisture from the pork just like you would the fat and it's much healthier.

Seasoning

Seasoning is a matter of personal taste. Some want just enough seasoning to tickle the taste buds, while others want their sausage hot enough to peel the skin off the roof of their mouths. It's your choice.

You have two options. Most grocery store chains carry at least one brand of sausage seasoning and the seasoning usually varies from mild to wild. My personal choice is the A.C. Legg

Legg brand, which is manufactured in Birmingham. If you have a problem locating pre-mixed seasoning at your grocery store, you may give A.C. Legg Co. a call at 205/324-3451.

The other choice is custom blending your own seasoning, which will take some experimenting. Black pepper, white pepper, paprika, cayenne, chili pepper, gumbo file, sage, mustard seed, thyme, rosemary, ginger, bay leaf, garlic salt, onion salt, fennel, nutmeg, celery seed, and peppercorns are popular ingredients for do-it-yourselfers.

One sausage-maker I know purchases big bottles of crushed, dried peppers (like you find on the tables at Pizza Hut) from Sam's Wholesale and uses that.

Whatever seasonings you choose, be sure to place them in a plastic bag and shake well to mix all ingredients.

The sausage-making process

Now that you have chosen your meat, your fat, the seasoning and the type of sausage, it's time to make some sausage. Follow these directions:

1. Start by cutting the venison and fat into cubes that will fit into the grinder. Place these in a plastic bag and place it in the freezer and leave it until it starts to freeze. This makes the sausage-making process much less messy.

2. Run the venison and the fat through the course plate separately.

3. Knead the venison and fat by hand, mixing thoroughly.

4. Run mixture through the medium plate.

Note: Seasoned venison sausage will keep only three months in the freezer, while unseasoned sausage will keep up to six months. If you are preparing enough sausage to last more than three months, you should freeze a potion of unseasoned sausage.

5. Spread sausage on a large sheet of waxed paper. Place the well-mixed seasoning in a shaker and shake evenly over sausage. Knead by hand again.

6. Run seasoned sausage through the fine plate.

7. If making patties, the sausage is ready. If making stuffed sausage, you must run sausage through again - with no plate - to stuff the casings.

Alabama's Wild Game

Woodchuck

How much wood could a woodchuck chuck if a woodchuck could chuck wood? That phrase is about all most Alabamians know about the woodchuck, or as he is more commonly known here, the groundhog.

The woodchuck is fairly common in Alabama, but rarely seen by most people. It lives in a burrow and forages in the forest eating plants and tender roots. If it is seen, it's usually when he pokes his head out of his burrow to scan its surroundings.

The woodchuck has meat that is dark and rich, and relatively tender and mild in flavor. There is no closed hunting season or limit on woodchuck in Alabama.

Alabama's Wild Game

Woodchuck recipes

Basic Fried Woodchuck

2 pounds woodchuck
1/2 cup milk
1 egg, beaten
Flour
Vegetable oil
Salt and pepper, to taste

Cut woodchuck into slices 1/2-inch thick. Mix beaten egg and milk. Salt and pepper woodchuck slices and dip into mixture; roll in flour. Place in hot oil and cook until golden brown, turning once.

Crock Pot Woodchuck

2 pounds woodchuck, cubed
1 large onion, quartered
2 packages Lipton Onion Soup mix
Salt and pepper, to taste
Garlic salt, to taste

Place in crock pot. Add onion soup mix, salt and pepper, garlic salt and onion. Fill crock pot half full of water, cover, and cook on medium heat. Serve over rice.

Woodchuck Casserole

2 pounds woodchuck, sliced thin
1/2 onion, chopped
1 tablespoon vegetable oil
1/2 teaspoon salt
Salt and pepper, to taste
4 large potatoes, sliced
1 can Campbell's Cream of Mushroom soup

Brown woodchuck slices in oil. Add salt and pepper. Slice potatoes and boil until tender. Drain. In a lightly greased baking dish, arrange layers of sliced potatoes, woodchuck and mushroom soup. Bake at 400 degrees for 35 minutes.

Woodchuck Meat Loaf

2 pounds woodchuck, ground
1 large onion, chopped
1 large tomato, chopped
4 tablespoons Dijon mustard
3 tablespoons jalapeno, crushed
2 tablespoons ground sage
2 eggs, beaten
1/3 cup Italian dressing
3/4 cup milk
1/2 teaspoon salt
1/2 teaspoon pepper

Mix all ingredients by hand in large bowl. Bake in loaf pan with foil on top for about 30 minutes at 350 degrees. Take foil off and bake 30 minutes until top is nicely browned and loaf is firm. Remove from oven and allow to cool for 15 minutes.

Alabama's Wild Game

Dressing woodchuck

Dressing a woodchuck is similar to dressing beaver and muskrat. Woodchuck may have a thick layer of fat in winter, but it doesn't have the disagreeable smell or taste like the fat found on those two animals. Hence, woodchuck doesn't need to be soaked in soda.

Begin (diagram No. 1) by cutting off the muskrat's feet (cuts No. 1 and No. 2) Make a cut from the anus to the throat (cut No. 3), being careful to cut only the pelt and not into the stomach cavity.

Flip the woodchuck over (diagram 2), and using a sharp skinning knife, continue to trim the pelt away from the meat. You may need to flip the muskrat back and forth until the pelt is trimmed completely away from the meat. Once the pelt is all the way off the body and pulled over the head, cut the head off and discard. Cut open the body cavity and remove the insides.

You may want to trim all fat. Cut the woodchuck into cooking-size pieces and he's ready to cook.

Alabama's Wild Game

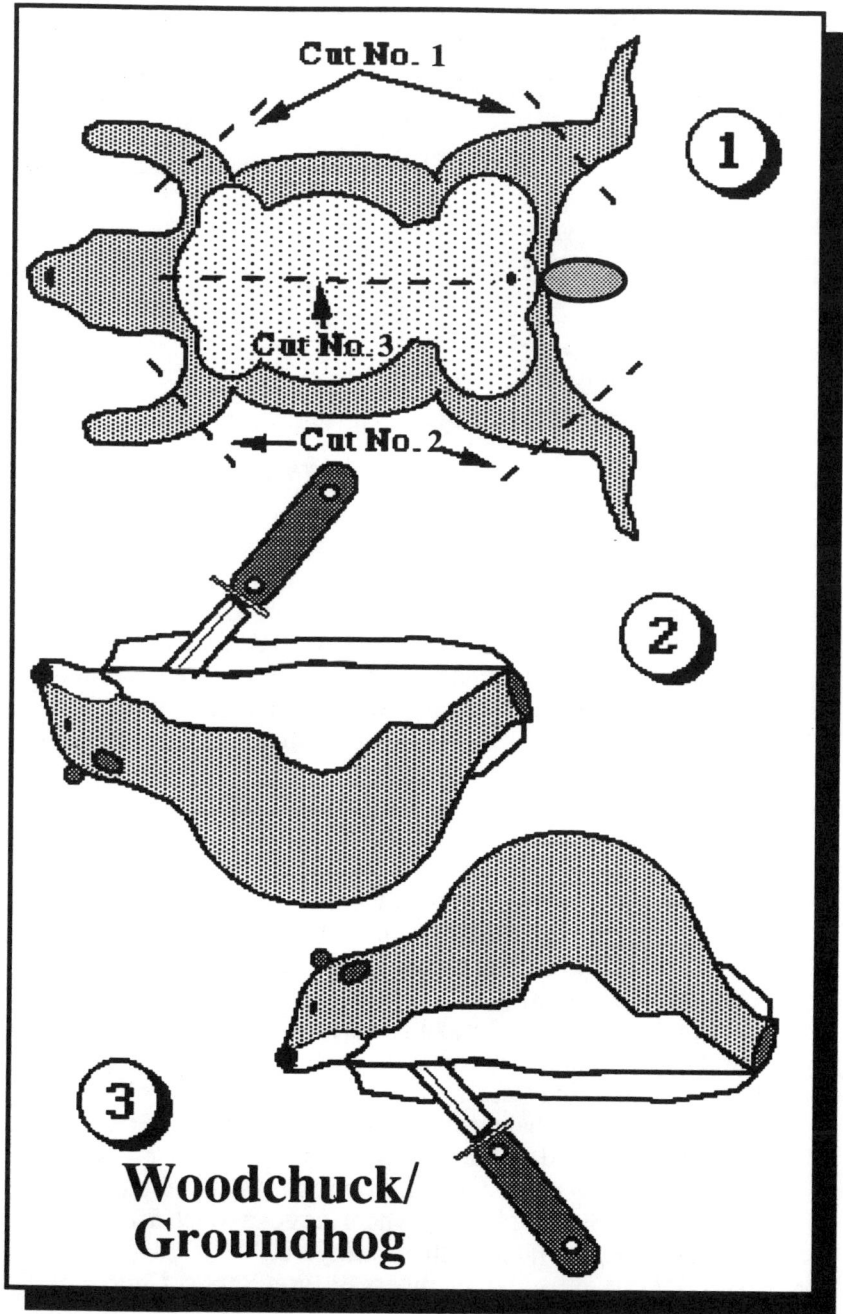

Woodchuck/ Groundhog

Alabama's Wild Game

About the author

Mike Bolton is a lifelong outdoorsman and outdoors editor of *The Birmingham News* since 1986. He has won numerous awards in that position, including the Governor's Award as Conservation Communicator of the Year. His package of stories on the quality of water in Alabama lakes was named as the top investigative story of the year by the Alabama Sportswriters Association in 1991 and was chosen as one of the Top 10 investigative stories in the nation by the Associated Press.

Bolton's first book, *The Complete Alabama Fisherman*, which was released in 1990, has become the handbook for fishermen in Alabama. It is now in its second printing.

Bolton's expertise in outdoors writing comes from experience. In January, 1992, he won the prestigious Buckmasters Classic, the top deer hunting event in the nation. He is also believed to be the only angler to have caught fish from every public lake in Alabama.

Bolton has fished in Alaska and Mexico and has hunted in Mexico, Colorado and all across the southeastern United States. His favorite hunting state is Alabama, however and his biggest thrill is cooking Alabama wild game for his family and friends.

Bolton is married to the former Elizabeth Rae Shryock, of Enterprise, and they have two children, Cory and Lauren. They live in Argo in St. Clair County where they can watch deer, wild turkey, rabbits and quail in their backyard.

The Boltons are active members of First Baptist Church of Springville.

Alabama's Wild Game

Also from Seacoast Books

The Complete Alabama Fisherman

All you need to know about fishing in Alabama, including:
• How the top anglers fish Alabama waters.
• Detailed fishing patterns, season by season, for every major Alabama body of water.
• Maps with fish holding structure for every major Alabama lake.
• Complete freshwater and saltwater fish dictionaries.
• More than 360 pages packed with information to make even the best fisherman better.

❑ Yes! I want The Complete Alabama Fisherman.

Name _____

Address _____

City, State, Zip _____

❑ Softbound............ $14.95
Add $1.95 per book for shipping and handling

Mail to: Seacoast Books
P.O. Box 26492
Birmingham, AL 35206

Alabama's Wild Game _____

Also from Seacoast Books

For the most
complete guide
to the fishes
of the Gulf of Mexico...

Dr. Bob Shipp's Fishes of the Gulf of Mexico

Scientifically accurate, yet written
in down-to-Earth language
with a sense of humor.

❑ **Yes! I want Dr. Bob Shipp's Fishes of the Gulf of Mexico.**

Name _____

Address _____

City, State, Zip _____

❑ Spiralbound or Perfectbound...........$16.95

Add $1.75 per book for shipping and handling

Mail to: Seacoast Books
P.O. Box 26492
Birmingham, AL 35206

Alabama's Wild Game

Alabama deer processors participating in Buckmasters Project Venison

Wholesale Meat
2203 Meridian St. N.
Huntsville, AL 35811
533-9744

Thompson's Meat Processing Co.
987 Halls Chapel Road
Alexandria, AL 36250
820-3138

Franklin County Processing
Rt. 1
Phil Campbell, AL 35581

P&B Meat Processing
Rt. 3 Box 1566
Pell City, AL 35125
672-2937

Scottsboro Meats
116 Chestnut St.
Scottsboro, AL 35768
574-2626

Peinhardt Processing
Hwy. 278 West
Cullman, AL 35055
734-9327

Oakland Farm Meats
1841 Highway 80
McIntyre Lane
Florence, AL 35645
764-0233

Terry Butts Meat Processing
Rt. 12
Blountsville, AL 35031
274-8247

Polar Meat & Locker
1129 4th Ave. North
Bessemer, AL 35020
425-2481

Mathews Meat Market
Hwy. 49 North
Lineville, AL 36364
396-5694

Billy's Deer Processing
Rt. 2 Box 538
Calera, AL 35040
663-2936

Reform Processing Plant
U.S. Hwy. 82 West
Reform, AL 35481
375-2319

Wesco Meat Processing
Rt. 2 Box 463-A
Altoona, AL 35952
589-2345

Acker Slaughter House
Rt. 1 Box 376
Buhl, AL 35446
339-0903

Alabama's Wild Game

Jerry's Processing
Main Street
West Blocton, AL 35184
425-8693

Clinton Grocery & Bait
Rt. 1 Box 24, Hwy. 14
West Greene, AL 35491

R&J Meat House
Hwy. 28 East
Livingston, AL 35470
652-7280 or 652-2489

York Ice Co.
205 Main St.
York, AL 36925
392-5138

Douglas Peteet
Rt. 1 Box 142 B
Demopolis, AL 36732
289-4919

Shiloh Butcher Shop
Rt. 1 Box 440
Dixons Mill, AL 36736
992-2444

Wayne's Custom Deer
P.O. Box 501
Camden, AL 36726
682-4777

Nichols Deer Processing
Jeff Davis Avenue
Selma, AL 36701
875-7121

Summerfield Quick Freeze
52 Dallas Road 277
Selma, AL 36701
872-7694

Reed's Quick Freeze
510 Dunlap Dr.
Clanton, AL 35054
755-5392

Deer Morgue
1486 Hwy 80 E.
Burkeville, AL 36052
284-1704

Taylor Meat Co.
1073 Bell St.
Montgomery, AL 36104
262-1822

Montgomery Meat Processors
2213 West Blvd.
Montgomery, AL 36108
263-2884

Deermasters
5760-A Kyser Court
Montgomery, AL 36116
288-0203

Mann's Meat Processors
Rt. 1 Box 185-AA
Wetumpka, AL 36092
567-4916

Benny Owens
103 Oak St.
Luverne, AL 36049
335-5151

Alabama's Wild Game

Murphy's Meat House
Rt. 6 Box 154
Troy, AL

Lawrence Adams
Rt. 2
Banks, AL
474-3237

Turner Deer Processing
4471 Co. Rd. 289
Lanett, AL 36852
644-3917

Bill's Deer Processing
Lee Road 169, Box 1023
Opelika, AL 36801
745-5495

Ray's Deer Processing
1740 Wright's Mill Road
Auburn, AL 36830
821-4829

Chamblee's Marina
120 Lee Road 802
Valley, AL 36854
749-5417

Seminole Meat Processing
3746 Opelika Road
Phenix City, AL 36867
298-1704

A.C.'s Video Grocery
864 Greenburt Road
Seale, AL 36875
855-3490

Driftwood General Store
Rt. 2 Box 65
Eufaula, AL 36027
687-3280

Enterprise Packing Corp.
Rt. 4 Box 746
Enterprise, AL 36330
347-8335

Crawford Meats
108 S. Doswell St.
Abbeville, AL 36310

Wiregrass Meat Processors
Rt. 3 Box 3
Headland, AL 36345
693-2717

Myers Meat Market
Highway 52 East
Columbia, AL 36319
794-2255

Southern Taxidermy
Rt. 1 Box 585
Grove Hill, AL 36451
275-8505

John E. Steadham
General Delivery
Stockton, AL 36579
937-5317

Farm Fresh Meats, Inc.
Hwy. 59 South
Robertsdale, AL 36507
947-7385

Alabama's Wild Game

Wilmer Dixie Dandy
Hwy. 98 & Wilmer Road
Wilmer, AL 36587
649-4647

Dawson's Country Smokehouse
16533 Dawson Road
Loxley, AL 36551
964-6978

J&R Meat Processing
398 Peachtree Road
Thomasville, AL 36784
636-2323

Hill Top Meat Co. Inc.
U.S. 29 North
Andalusia, AL 36420
388-2393

Richardson Meat Inc.
3706 Greensboro Ave.
Tuscaloosa, AL 35403
759-1563